Walt Disney's

GOOFY

THE GOOD SPORT

THE GOOD SPORT

HPBooks®

First published in the United States in 1985 by HPBooks, Inc.,

P. O. Box 5367, Tucson, AZ 85703 (602/888-2150)

ISBN: 0-89586-414-2

Library of Congress Catalog Card
Number: 85-60488

Created, designed and produced by
Three Duck Editions Ltd.
(Justin Knowles Publishing Group),
P. O. Box 99, Exeter, Devon, England

For Three Duck Editions:
Text: Flora O'Brien
Research: Christopher Fagg and Justin Knowles
Editors: Margaret Daykin and Charlotte Parry-Crooke
Design: David Pearce
Production: Nick Facer

For HPBooks:
Publisher: Rick Bailey
Editorial Director: Randy Summerlin
Editors: Jim Barrett and Judith Schuler

Typeset by P & M Typesetting Ltd, Exeter, England
Printed and bound in Hong Kong by Mandarin Offset Ltd

Notice: The information in this book is true and complete to
the best of our knowledge. All recommendations are made
without guarantee on the part of the author or HPBooks.
The author and publisher disclaim all liability in connection
with the use of this information.

First American edition

CONTENTS

PREFACE 6

INTRODUCTION 7

THE EVOLUTION OF THE GOOF 8
GOOFY JOINS THE GANG
GOOFY BECOMES A GOOD FRIEND
GOOFY'S BIG BREAK

GOOFY'S RISE TO STARDOM 18
A FULL MEMBER OF THE TEAM
A STARRING ROLE — WITH WILBUR
GOOFY AT THE CROSSROADS
WARTIME INTERLUDE

GOOFY INTO THE POST-WAR PERIOD 44
GOOFY: FORTIES FAVORITE
MR. SUBURBAN MAN — GOOFY IN THE FIFTIES

GOOFY AND THE WORLD 56
GOOFY'S LIFESTYLE
GOOFY'S WARDROBE
ROMANTIC PURSUITS

BRINGING GOOFY TO LIFE 66
ANIMATING GOOFY
TEACHING AN OLD DAWG NEW TRICKS

GOOFY FOR SALE 76
MERCHANDISING GOOFY
GOOFY IN PRINT

RETURN OF THE GOOF 88
GOOFY TODAY
SPORT GOOFY — A SURE WINNER

FILMOGRAPHY 94

BIBLIOGRAPHY 95

SPORT GOOFY DIARY 96

WELL —
I'LL BE
DURNED!

PREFACE

Walt Disney's *Goofy — The Good Sport* is a deservedly popular subject for the second volume in this Series, which commenced with Walt Disney's *Donald Duck — 50 Years of Happy Frustration*. We know that Goofy's many admirers will be with us in thinking it is high time that he be saluted in this way. He has sustained and strengthened his unique character to emerge as one of the most endearing and enduring of the early Disney characters. And his career has now taken off in a new extension of an old interest — sports.

Goofy's latest involvement promises rich rewards and further entertainment for all of us. Because, however straight-forward a situation may seem, once Goofy becomes actively involved he is drawn into the most impossible complications. We also know that whatever happens to him, he will bear no malice, and experience neither embarrassment nor injured pride. Goofy is the eternal optimist, always willing to "have a go."

Like all good clowns, however, Goofy has greater perception and sensitivity than may first be apparent. Perhaps this is the secret of his continuing appeal. He is the good guy who keeps on trying and — who knows — he may succeed one day.

His charming habit of "dressing for the part" reflects the hidden actor in us all and distinguishes him from others in the gang. Goofy is not an exhibitionist, nor is he compensating for secret inhibitions. He simply throws himself wholeheartedly into every new challenge — and who can say a word against that?

Despite his uncomplicated approach to life, Goofy's character is not easy to rationalize. And that made me all the more eager to try — like Goofy. Wayne Morris and Bob Ogden of Walt Disney Productions will remember their initial bemusement, during my visit to New York in early 1984, at my attempts to articulate the need for this closer look at Goofy.

Our team, led by Christopher Fagg, Charlotte Parry-Crooke, David Pearce, Maggie Daykin, Flora O'Brien and Michelle Barnacle, joins me in thanking Walt Disney Productions and David R. Smith, the Director of the Walt Disney Archives, for their generous cooperation. Without them, a book like this could never have been published. Our thanks, too, to T.B. Boyd, Wendall Mohler, Wayne Morris, Greg Crosby, Carson Van Osten, David Cleghorn, Paula Sigman, Rose Motzko and all at Burbank for their assistance and support. We are also indebted to Keith Bales, managing director of Walt Disney Productions Ltd., for his initiative and sustained encouragement. In addition, we thank our co-publishers for their commitment, encouragement and enthusiasm for this project from its conception to its realization.

Finally, our thanks to Goofy, who symbolizes friendship, optimism, humor, honesty and loyalty — qualities that most of us admire and would wish to emulate. Goofy, you are a great pal and a good sport!

Justin Knowles
Three Duck Editions
London, 1985

INTRODUCTION

Goofy, the big shambling guy with the dog's head and toothy grin, is the mystery man of the Disney group. Even his official Studio biography has to admit defeat when it comes to accounting for his early life and times. It states flatly that "like Topsy, he just growed." All one can say for certain is for a few years he was just sort of around. Then he progressed to bit parts in Mickey Mouse pictures before finally achieving stardom in his own right in *Goofy and Wilbur* (1939).

Along the way, Goofy appeared in some of the greatest Disney shorts of the 1930s. His subsequent solo film career lasted for many years: from 1938 to 1965. In addition, he became one of the best-known international Disney comic-book characters. Not bad for a good-natured bonehead who never did anything right if he could get it wrong.

And now — at a time when Mickey and Donald represent a classic past — Goofy has taken on a new lease of life. As a remarkably contemporary figure — Sport Goofy — he is currently encouraging young people to take a thoroughly positive attitude towards sports, health and fitness.

Goofy, then, is a many-sided, fascinating character we would like to know more about. But where should we start our investigation? One thing is certain, Goofy is the last person to ask. He's far too modest to think of himself as anything more than an ordinary guy who's been lucky enough to have a good life at the top without ever having to be false to his own good-natured self.

So, what can we say about the Goof? First and foremost, Goofy is firmly established in the tradition of silent comedy stars such as Chaplin, Keaton and Harold Lloyd. Like those great comics, Goofy uses all his skills as an acrobat and mime to entertain us. His physical awkwardness is more apparent than real. When we watch him undertake the simplest task, we know that he will get it wrong — sublimely, hopelessly, complicatedly wrong — just as we know he has complete confidence in his ability to get it right. And what if he does continually bump against the mysteriously resistant nature of the world and the objects in it? For Goofy it is, and always will be, a world of discovery.

Goofy is also essentially a rural clown whose simple-mindedness is a rich source of humor in his films and comic-book adventures. If Mickey is a plucky Tom Sawyer, always ready with a smart solution to painting a fence, then Goofy is a Huckleberry Finn. He is part of an American tradition in which simple country cunning can be more than a match for oversmart city slickers. Reason enough to turn back the clock to when it all began and take a closer look at the inimitable, undefeatable Goofy.

THE EVOLUTION OF THE GOOF

GOOFY JOINS THE GANG

Dippy Dawg and the gang — Donald Duck, Mickey Mouse, Horace Horsecollar, Minnie Mouse, Clarabelle Cow and Pluto. A rural family group as they all appeared around 1935.

Tracing Goofy's career from its beginnings brings us up against elements of the mystery that seems to be part of his life, art, character and career. According to his Studio biography, Goofy "just growed." But on digging deep into the archives, we learn the following factual details.

In 1932, Walt Disney received an Academy Award for creating Mickey Mouse. Columnist Louella Parsons wrote that, as a movie personality, Mickey weighed in "with a bigger screen following than nine-tenths of the stars in Hollywood." In 1933, Mickey's fifth birthday was the occasion of the razzmatazz reserved for national heroes, such as Charles Lindbergh.

From the front cover of *Time* magazine to the *Woman's Home Companion*, from *The New Yorker* to the *Journal of Aesthetics and Art Criticism*, the Mickey Mouse phenomenon was reported and analyzed in unprecedented detail. Overwhelmingly, the verdict was ecstatic. The trade newspaper *Motion Picture Daily* spoke for all: "When you say it is up to the Mickey Mouse Disney standard, there is nothing left to be said."

Now that Mickey was a full-fledged star, there was an urgent need to create vehicles for him. He would have to have friends and acquaintances to inhabit his

9

Left: Goofy — then known as Dippy Dawg — makes his bow in his first picture, *Mickey's Revue* (1932). Despite side whiskers and pince-nez, the hat and vest clearly point to an evolving Goofy.

cartoon universe and reflect aspects of his personality. Minnie had been with him from the beginning, and in 1930, a playful pup called Pluto joined them. At the same time, Clarabelle Cow and Horace Horsecollar emerged from a menagerie of barnyard characters to become their friends.

Then Goofy joined the gang. Originally, he was a lazy good-for-nothing named Dippy Dawg. As Dippy, he was first glimpsed briefly (and heavily in disguise) as a member of the audience in the black-and-white cartoon, *Mickey's Revue* (1932). Goofy didn't do anything except laugh. But that laugh — on loan to Goofy courtesy of its owner, ex-circus clown and musician Pinto Colvig — was memorable enough for Walt Disney to notice. A few months later, the laugh, and the Goof-to-be, were featured in a Mickey Mouse short called *The Whoopee Party*. As senior Disney storyman Steve Hulett recalls:

"He helped Mickey prepare party eats in the kitchen, and he did it without a hitch.

Right and below:
Sweet smell of
success — Goofy as
Hollywood star in *The
Goofy Success Story,* a
1955 television
celebration of his
career.

His characteristic klutziness and naiveté had not yet been fully discovered. In the later *Mickey's Birthday Party* (1942) he was able to destroy a kitchen, cake and party single-handed, all with perfect innocence and good humor."

Much later, in the television biography *The Goofy Success Story* (1955), we're given a different account of our hero's rise to fame. Apparently, he was "discovered" not by Disney, but by Hollywood talent scouts alerted by his famous "ahunh-ahunh-ahunh" laugh in a theater audience. This version continues that Dippy was signed by a big studio and went through the traditional Hollywood star-making machine. As so often happens to talented newcomers, one of the first changes was to give him a zappier name — goodbye Dippy Dawg, hello Goofy!

Which version should we believe? Screen biographies are often unreliable and prone to overglamorize their heroes. But if neither account gives the full story, how *did* Dippy Dawg become Dippy the Goof, then Goofy?

For the answers, we have to imagine ourselves back in the early days of Mickey Mouse. These were the days of the Great Depression, when Mickey and his friends lived, poor but happy, in the run-down back country of Missouri, where Walt Disney himself as a child had lived on a farm between 1906 and 1910. It was a barnyard world of make-do-and-mend, of hand-me-down clothes, patched-up shacks and gimcrack machinery.

The story began when Walt Disney discovered Mickey and brought him and his world to the big screen. Walt had a favorite word to describe the funny, funky comedy that happened around Mickey. That word was *goofy*. It meant a funny, innocent, screwy, flip-flop, harmless rural slapstick. That being so, it's probably not too much to say that Goofy came into existence as a representative spirit of the rural world Mickey inhabited.

Mickey himself was probably quicker than most to see that Dippy Dawg only *seemed* to be a dumb hick — in reality he was Goofy all along. For Mickey, heading toward superstardom, Dippy/Goofy remained a nostalgic, vital link with his country roots and the embodiment of rural innocence and integrity.

Below: In *Mickey's Fire Brigade* (1935), genteel Clarabelle Cow receives a shock to her modesty. Slapstick scenes became less common in Disney cartoon shorts as Hollywood studios were subjected to pressure from overly zealous guardians of public morality. Here, Goofy and Donald have not yet achieved their familiar cartoon forms.

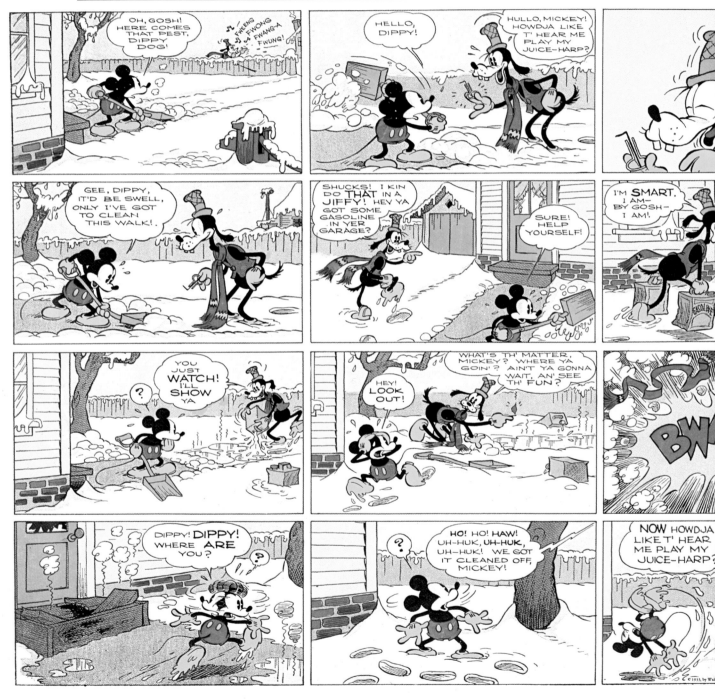

While Mickey was pursuing his screen career, Goofy was content to remain in the background. Ambition was not part of his personality makeup and, when he did become more widely known, it was through the Mickey Mouse comic strips. From 1933 on he gradually emerged in the strips as a neighbor and occasional associate of Mickey in his activities.

Unkind eyes might have seen the Dippy/Goofy character of this period as a no-account lazybones with no visible means of support. Yet fate was waiting for him in the person of comic-strip genius Floyd Gottfredson, who had taken over the syndicated Mickey Mouse daily newspaper comic strips in 1932.

The needs of the daily and weekly Mickey Mouse strips quickly exhausted the stories and situations from the films. So over the next few years, therefore, Gottfredson and his team of writers and artists sent Mickey and his friends on many exciting and original adventures. To

serve the demand of plot and character development, Gottfredson began to organize his stories around a small group of central characters. These included Mickey, Minnie, the villainous Peg Leg Pete, the feisty Donald Duck — and Goofy, whose slow-burning brain and genius for doing the wrong thing made him a natural sidekick for the quick-witted Mickey.

In the process, Goofy's personality began to blossom. He gradually lost his barnyard-animal look and became almost human. At the same time his previously hidden qualities of loyalty and good-natured imperturbability came to the fore. Gradually, Mickey began to rely on Goofy and Donald as boon companions on his quests into a fast-paced, exciting and sometimes dangerous world. (See also pages 82-86.)

Left: Goofy appeared as Dippy Dawg in newspaper comic strips beginning in 1933. As a character, Dippy was more boisterous (and more irritating) than Goofy. This typical Dippy Dawg strip story was originally published on January 8, 1933.

Below: Peg Leg Pete, perennial villain of Mickey Mouse cartoons and comic strips, throws a scare into Dippy Dawg. As Dippy changed his appearance over the years, Pete later "grew" a proper leg in place of the wood one. One explanation was that comic-strip artists who drew Pete found it hard to remember whether his wood leg should be on the right or left!

Right: The young Art Babbitt, holding a clipboard, is pictured on the right. With him in this 1932 photograph are, left to right, Wilfred Jackson, Walt Disney and Ted Sears.

While Goofy was maturing into a fully rounded character in the comic strips, the Disney Studio was taking the world by storm. Of all the animation studios working in the 1920s and early 1930s, it was the Disney Studio that became known for originality, humor, pace of story development, and a magical ability to impart personality and pathos to its cartoon characters. In addition, Disney and his Studio made an impact with purely technical innovations. Walt was the first to produce a cartoon with a fully synchronized sound track (*Steamboat Willie*, 1928) and the first to use the new three-color Technicolor process (in *Flowers and Trees*, 1932).

Inside and outside the world of professional animators, it was agreed that the Disney Studio was the place where the most interesting things were happening. As a result, Disney attracted the best and brightest of a young generation of artists, animators and story men.

The elation and intensity of those days is vividly recalled by two Disney veterans of the period, Frank Thomas and Ollie Johnston in their definitive account, *Disney Animation: The Illusion of Life*, published in 1981:

"Exciting new things were happening all around us and this close personal contact and the crazy associations kept us stimulated. We were all trying to outdo each other in thinking of screwy actions, deliberately trying to be different, to be funnier, to come up with an unexpected gag in everything we did — away from the Studios as well as at work."

In 1933, the years of hard work culminated in the blockbusting cartoon *Three Little Pigs*, which confirmed Disney in the public mind as the leading exponent of the animated film. Today, it is difficult to convey just how great the impact of this film was. Its theme tune, "Who's Afraid of the Big Bad Wolf?," was a national hit, in its jaunty optimism, and caught the spirit of a people determined to overcome the specter of the Depression.

One of the animators who worked on *Three Little Pigs* was Art Babbitt. He originally worked out of New York and had been one of the highest-paid animators on the East Coast. Some idea of Walt Disney's impact and reputation can be gained from Babbitt's 1932 decision to give up his East Coast career, move to California and offer to work for Walt Disney — for nothing! "I'll work for you for free for three months," Babbitt told Disney. "After that you can fire me — or pay me what I'm worth."

Art Babbitt's arrival was to prove a vital step forward in Goofy's screen career. Babbitt gave the Goof the break he was ready for — a recognition of his enormous potential. Some 50 years later, Babbitt's memory of his first encounter with Goofy is crystal clear:

Left: *Three Little Pigs* (1933) was the film that sealed the Disney Studio's dominance over the animated cartoon. The film's theme tune, "Who's Afraid of the Big Bad Wolf?," became a national hit in Depression-era America. The cartoon combined elements of story, drama, humor and personality in new and exciting ways — an approach that generated classic Mickey Mouse, Goofy and Donald cartoons of the mid-to-late 1930s.

"The first time I came across Goofy was in a black-and-white short called *Mickey's Service Station* (1935). In that picture, Goofy was on top of an engine block and, as he reached down into it, his own hand came up behind him and goosed him. Then there was a bit of monkey business before he found out it was his own hand.

"I wanted that scene very badly because I thought I could have fun with it. But they had only allotted, I think… 7½ or 8 feet of film for the whole business. I thought you couldn't do anything in that. At any rate, I almost had to beg for that scene. Finally, I made a deal with Disney that I would work on a sequence for Peg Leg Pete, a character I detest. In return, I could have the Goofy thing to do.

"Well, the Goofy thing wound up 57 feet long and after that I was always kidded about padding scenes. I *never* pad 'em. I just play 'em out."

Art Babbitt was the person most responsible for lifting Goofy out of the bit-player category and setting him on the road to star billing. Writing in 1934 he put it this way:

"In my opinion, the Goof hitherto has been a weak cartoon character because both his physical and mental make-up were indefinite and intangible… the only characteristic which formerly identified itself with him was his voice. No effort was made to endow him with appropriate business to do, a set of mannerisms or a mental attitude."

More recently Babbitt has summarized it thus: "Goofy originally was a sort of stock character in most scenes, but nobody had attempted to do anything with him. I can't say that I created Goofy, but I was the first one to build him up and give him a character!" How Babbitt achieved this breakthrough is detailed overleaf.

NO SMOKE FROM CIGAR

This Studio artists' reference model sheet for *Mickey's Service Station* (1935) incorporates elements of the film: Peg Leg Pete in threatening pose, a nervous Goofy and an equally jumpy Mickey, as well as the bucking-bronco engine of Pete's car, which breaks free at the end of the film and chases Pete over the horizon.

GOOFY'S RISE TO STARDOM
A FULL MEMBER OF THE TEAM

The years 1933 to 1940 saw a Golden Age at the Disney Studio. During this time, Disney assembled a team once described as "being capable of creating the animation equivalent of Chartres Cathedral." It was not simply that Disney artists drew better than those working for the other animation studios, nor that the stories were better or the gags were funnier than those of other companies. It was more that the Studio, having mastered all the technical aspects of animation, was free to think about the personalities of its cartoon characters. There was time to ponder the reasons why Goofy and his pals did the things they did and to ask how they would react in any given situation.

Disney animators thought about their cartoon characters in the same way as an actor prepares for a role. They tried to discover the true spirit and motivation of each one. This process of preparation was based on an intense observation of human and animal movements and behavior. The following excerpts are taken from Art Babbitt's own character analysis of the Goof. Written in 1935, it provides a fine example of this kind of thinking.

"Think of the Goof as a composite of an everlasting optimist, a gullible Good Samaritan, a half-wit, and a shiftless, good-natured hick. He is loose-jointed and gangly, but not rubbery. He can move fast if he has to, but would rather avoid any overexertion, so he takes what seems the easiest way.

"No matter what happens, he accepts it finally as being for the best, or at least amusing. He is willing to help anyone and offers his assistance, even where he is not needed and just creates confusion. He very seldom, if ever, reaches his objective or completes what he has started... Any little distraction can throw him off his train of thought...

"His posture is nil. His back arches the wrong way, and his little stomach protrudes. His head, stomach and knees lead his body. His neck is quite long and scrawny. His knees sag, and his feet are large and flat. He walks on his heels, and his toes turn up. His shoulders are narrow and slope rapidly, giving the upper part of his body a thinness and making his arms seem long and heavy, though actually not drawn that way. His hands are very sensitive and expressive, and though his gestures are broad, they should still reflect the gentleman.

"Never think of the Goof as a sausage with rubber-hose attachments. Though he is very flexible and floppy, his body still has a solidity and weight...

"The Goof's head can be thought of in terms of a caricature of a person with a pointed dome — large, dreamy eyes, buck teeth and a weak chin, a large mouth, a thick lower lip, a fat tongue and a bulbous nose that grows larger on its way out and turns up...

"He is very bashful, yet when something very stupid has befallen him, he mugs the camera like an amateur actor with

Walt Disney, Mickey Mouse and staff at the Disney Studio in Summer 1932. The Studio, then on Hyperion Avenue in Hollywood, was the cradle of the enormously successful Disney output during the 1930s. Young Walt is to Mickey's right. Behind him, on his right, is Pinto Colvig, Goofy's "voice." To Colvig's right, in suit and tie, perches snazzily dressed Art Babbitt, transplanted from the East Coast. Babbitt gave Goofy his first screen break in *Moving Day* (1936). Standing to the right is Floyd Gottfredson, comic-strip artist. Framed in the open doorway is the tall figure of Jack Kinney, who gave Goofy a new lease on life in 1940.

relatives in the audience, trying to cover up his embarrassment by making faces and signaling to them. "He is in close contact with sprites, goblins, fairies and other such fantasia. Each object or piece of mechanism, which to us is lifeless, has a soul and personality in the mind of the Goof. The improbable becomes real where the Goof is concerned."

To express this complex character in action, Babbitt devised an approach in which, as he cheerfully admits, he broke every rule of animation there was. He invented a weird and wonderful walk for Goofy — in which every step represented a miniature encyclopedia of the humanly impossible — and harmonized it into a floppy, loose-limbed shuffle that owed more than a little to the style of the black entertainers of the time.

Mickey's Service Station (1935) marked the first appearance of the fully developed screen Goofy, and it set the pattern for the cartoon shorts of the next few years. In this short, Mickey, Donald and Goofy star as the repair crew you'd least like to have work on your car.

They find themselves working against the clock on a rush job for the villainous bully, Peg Leg Pete. Pete's snazzy roadster has developed a squeak, but he's sure the trio can complete the task of fixing it without any need to invoke Pete's own brand of penalty clause — which seems to involve a degree of assault and battery.

With a *High Noon*-style sense of anxiety nicely established, our heroes set to work stripping down Pete's pride and joy, while we sit on the edge of our seats, fully confident of impending disaster. As Mickey removes the wheels and Donald unravels the radiator grill as though it were a piece of knitting, it seems increasingly likely the machinery will be harder to put together than take apart.

Amid mounting urgency to meet the

Goofy gingerly searches inside the engine block of Pete's car for the source of an unidentifiable squeak in *Mickey's Service Station* (1935).

deadline, Goofy's sequence with the cylinder block increases the tension with the sheer maddening slowness of his reactions as he reaches cautiously into one cylinder after the other in search of the mysterious squeak. His hand — now mysteriously imbued with a life of its own — emerges from beneath the block and prods his own rear end. With rare cunning, Goofy surreptitiously palms a hammer in his other hand and smashes it down onto the interloper. Ouch!

Finally, the cause of the squeak is revealed among the ruins of the car — a cricket (the inspiration for Goofy's pal, Wilbur, perhaps?) — and a frantic, doomed struggle to reassemble the pieces begins. Though far from safe, the car is almost in one piece when Pete, Mephistopheles-like, comes to claim it — only to have it explode the moment he tries to drive it away. A furiously revving engine whizzes out of the wreckage and chases Pete down the road and over the horizon.

Mickey's Service Station is a fine example of the Studio's mastery of the short comedy cartoon, setting its gags and comic antics in the context of a race against time. For Babbitt's Goofy, it marks a full integration as a comic character. Goofy is now as fully animated, as "alive," as Mickey and Donald, but while they speed the action up, he slows the tempo down by getting wholly involved in minor matters. Babbitt's great achievement was to make

this useful comic device believable as an aspect of Goofy's *personality*. Goofy is *not* stupid or thoughtless. In fact, he thinks longer and harder than most. *Then* he gets it wrong.

Art Babbitt's Goofy was a hit with the movie-going public. More screen roles followed in cartoons with Mickey and Donald. In these films Goofy often encounters inanimate objects which spring into life and enmesh him in their toils. For Goofy, such events occasion surprise and interest rather than fear or aggression.

In *Moving Day* (1936), for instance, Goofy is an ice delivery man who finds Mickey and Donald in the midst of a daylight flit from their house. The rent is overdue, and the landlord has sent the sheriff with a warrant to confiscate the furniture in lieu of payment.

Good-natured Goofy agrees to help load the furniture into his ice wagon. At this point a piano takes on a mischievous life of its own in a classic sequence, animated by Art Babbitt, which develops into an epic struggle between the rational and the irrational. It seems the piano doesn't want to leave home. When Goofy pushes it up the ramp and onto the wagon, the piano waits until his back is turned before serenely gliding down the ramp and back into the house.

Goofy being Goofy, this happens several times before his brain registers all is not well. A dim but growing awareness dawns that a degree of strategy and cunning may be required to defeat this unexpectedly formidable opponent. Goofy elaborately pantomimes indifference, only to whirl around to catch the piano frozen in the act of escape. The closely fought duel of wills continues as Goofy slyly lurks by the back door and peeks around to find the delinquent piano mimicking his action.

At last the piano seems quiescent and Goofy turns his back to continue with his next task. With lightning acceleration, the piano careens back into the house, leaving a flattened Goofy in its wake.

This brilliantly staged and paced sequence illustrates Goofy's ability to step effortlessly from one time frame to another. At one moment he is engaged in the purposeful actions of adulthood, and the next he has escaped into the magical, play-filled world of early childhood.

Goofy is romantic and innocent. His absurdly articulated frame is always two beats behind or ahead of the action. He is forever treading on the step that isn't

In *Moving Day* (1936), Goofy meets a piano that doesn't want to leave home! Several efforts to get it into the truck end with the piano tiptoeing back into the house. Animator Art Babbitt's brilliant sequence culminates with the piano making one last determined dash for home base — flattening poor Goofy in the process.

Right: Goofy on the wrong end of a harpoon gun in *The Whalers* (1938).

Left: Goofy, Donald and Mickey crack a rib or two in *Boat Builders* (1938).

there — and falling into a timeless world that is all his own.

The shorts of this period, from 1936 to 1938, established Goofy, along with Mickey and Donald, as a full member of the front-running team of Disney characters. Goofy's infinite capacity for slow-motion chaos, combined with his invincible good humor, made him the perfect stooge. Donald — a duck of uncertain temper but unquenchable spirit — could be relied upon to inject bursts of furious energy. Mickey was always the can-do leader. These three "mouseketeers" starred together in many cartoon shorts, including *Moose Hunters* (1937), *Clock Cleaners* (1937), *Lonesome Ghosts* (1937), *The Whalers* (1938) and *Boat Builders* (1938).

In *Moose Hunters* (1937), Goofy and Donald — seemingly anticipating Woody Allen's Mr. and Mrs. Berkowitz — dress up in a moose outfit to lure their prey to where Mickey, in full hunting gear waits for the moose with a loaded gun. But there's no moose for the Mouse until Goofy uncorks a bottle of essence of "Miss Moose." The heady fumes waft across the forest, then turn into delicate hands that caress the face of a bull moose and lead him hypnotized to the glade where Donald and Goofy wait disguised.

With a brisk slap of the cheeks, the phantom hands that led him awake the bull moose. Aflame with passion, he opens his eyes and finds himself being vamped by the Goofy-Donald moose act. When Goofy suddenly finds himself momentarily without his moose suit, he keeps the bull at bay by performing a coy bubble dance with the aid of a convenient bush.

A different sort of peek-a-boo game is the highlight of *Lonesome Ghosts,* made in

Below: Goofy and Donald encounter an unappreciative audience for their moose act in *Moose Hunters* (1937).

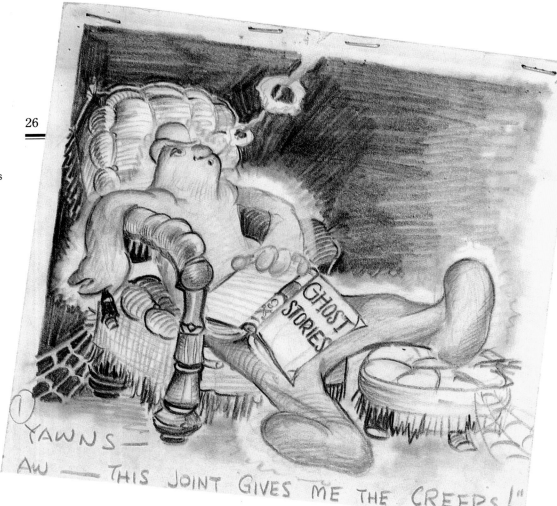

Right: Tough-guy ghost from *Lonesome Ghosts* (1937) ponders how to bring some excitement into his "life."

the same year. Ghostbusters Mickey, Donald and Goofy are called in to sort out a bad case of multiple haunting. The twist of the story is they've been called in by the spooks themselves, a rough crew, who are bored with having nobody to frighten.

When they enter the haunted mansion, the trio split up. First Mickey, then Donald, are subjected to a rapid series of ghostly slapstick gags. Goofy's sequence follows and helps slow down the tempo. Catching sight of a ghostly figure in a dresser mirror, Goofy — naturally — assumes it is his own reflection. "Gawrsh," he says, "I never know'd I was so handsome."

But something about the image arouses his suspicions. He peers into the mirror and begins an elaborate series of movements and expressions designed to catch out the reflection. The ghost faithfully mimics every movement and adds

a few of his own. Here, the comedy turns on the fact that Goofy can make us believe in the impeccable morality of his approach. He is, after all, prepared to give the reflection the benefit of the doubt. In the event, it is the ghost that gets bored with the game first and chases Goofy into the dresser drawers. In a slam-bang climax, the dresser — with Goofy still in it — slides down the stairs into a kitchen cabinet that dumps a gooey mixture of flour, eggs and molasses on the intrepid ghostbusters. As the trio rise from the floor, completely coated with white goo, the roughneck spooks arrive to have the last laugh — but are stopped dead (so to speak) in their tracks by the sight of the gooey ghostbusters. With a haunting cry of "G-g-ghosts!," the real ghosts, scared out of their wits, head for the hills.

Lonesome Ghosts, like the other

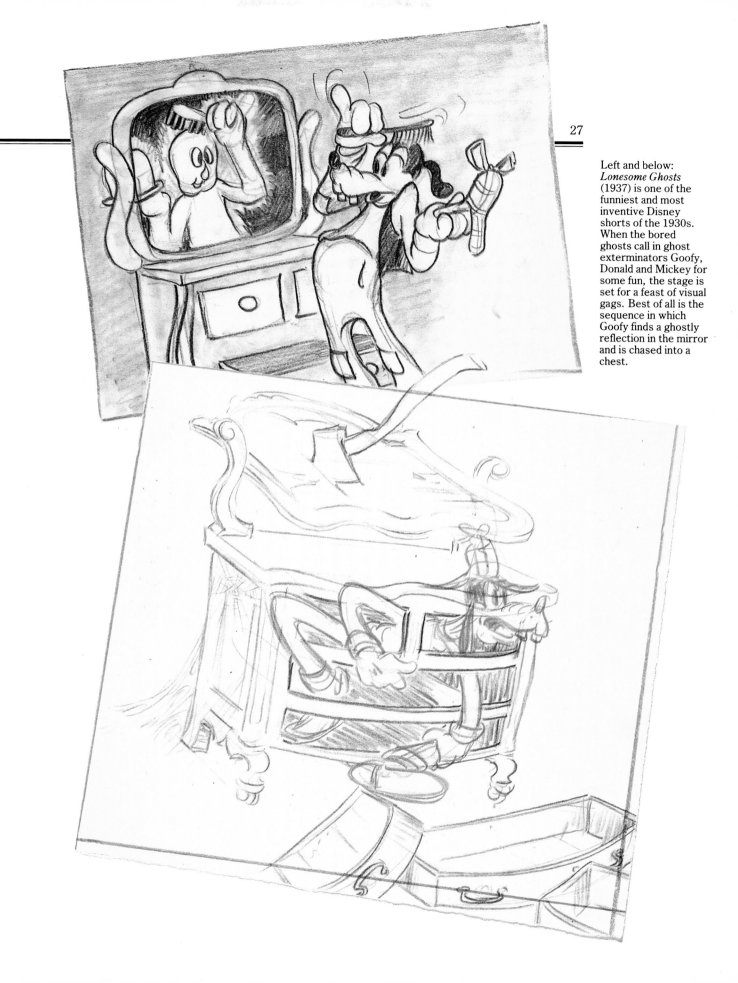

Left and below:
Lonesome Ghosts
(1937) is one of the
funniest and most
inventive Disney
shorts of the 1930s.
When the bored
ghosts call in ghost
exterminators Goofy,
Donald and Mickey for
some fun, the stage is
set for a feast of visual
gags. Best of all is the
sequence in which
Goofy finds a ghostly
reflection in the mirror
and is chased into a
chest.

Right: In *Clock Cleaners* (1937), Goofy finds himself gonged out and (far right) very close to the edge 100 stories high! Goofy's acrobatic talents recall Harold Lloyd's exploits — underlining the debt owed by 1930s comedy cartoons to silent comedies of the 1920s.

cartoons of the mid- to late 1930s, was animated in the Studio's grandest manner. The colors are soft and glowing, while the figures seem to flow effortlessly through the action. *Clock Cleaners* (1937), in particular, achieves a dreamlike storybook effect that echoes the atmosphere of Geppetto's Workshop in *Pinocchio* (1940). Mickey, Goofy and Donald are discovered on top of a dizzily high clock tower. As they begin their cleaning operations, Donald loses no time in getting into serious trouble with a sinister clock spring. Mickey has a tug-of-war with a sleepily uncooperative stork.

However, it is Goofy who steals the show in an extraordinary sequence that is really a film within a film, culminating in an extended spoof of a 1920s Harold Lloyd cliffhanger. A dazed Goofy walks off the ledge of the tower only to be snatched from disaster by a series of fortuitous hooks, pulleys and flagpoles.

Clearly, Goofy was on his way up — and in more senses than one. His appeal was to earn him more of the action in future roles.

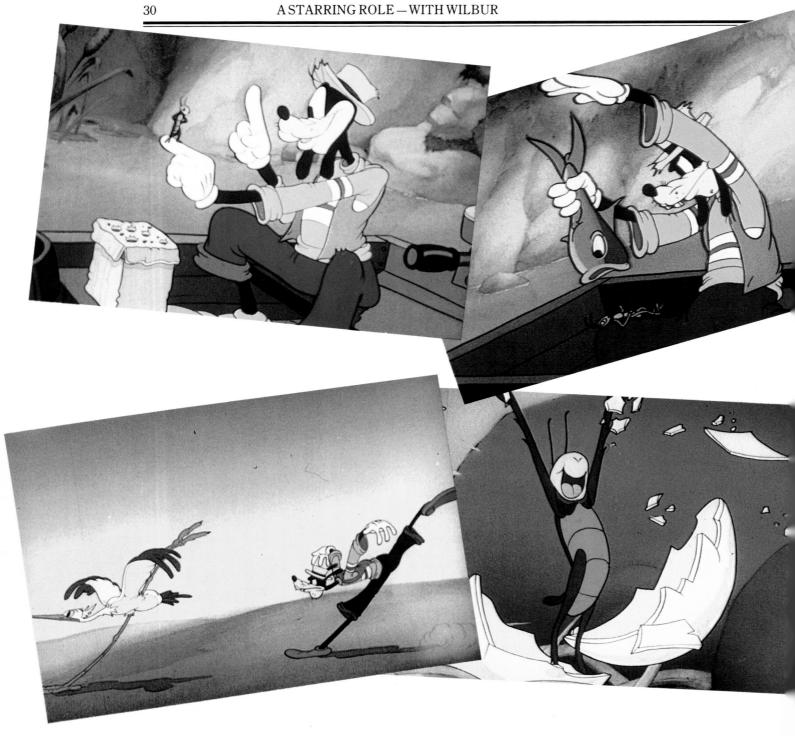

On the strength of his performances with Mickey and Donald, Goofy received the accolade of a solo starring role in *Goofy and Wilbur* (1939). In this 8-minute short, Goofy goes fishing with his pugnacious and resourceful grasshopper companion, Wilbur.

The movie is a miniature drama of loss and restitution, played out against an idyllic background of lake and shore. Brave Goofy rescues his friend from the jaws of a giant fish, only to see him be swallowed by a frog which, in turn, is eaten by a stork. Ever loyal, Goofy never gives up hope of rescue throughout the exciting chase sequence that follows. Despite Goofy's optimism, we fear the worst when the bird flies away.

Goofy mourns his friend, and in a fantasy sequence we see an angelic Wilbur entering the Pearly Gates. However, all is resolved in a surprise ending: Wilbur, very much alive, pops triumphantly out of an egg in the stork's nest.

Goofy and Wilbur (1938) marked Goofy's first screen appearance as a solo star. Teamed with his pal Wilbur — a tough and resourceful grasshopper — Goofy goes on a fishing trip with more than one catch in it. Minor crisis arises when Wilbur is swallowed by a fish — fortunately Goofy is on hand to rescue him. But when accident-prone Wilbur is eaten by a frog, which is swallowed by a stork, Goofy — even at his most determined — gets left behind. Eventually Wilbur turns up, in cracking form, inside a stork's egg, and the two pals are reunited at last.

Below right: The essential screen Goofy of the 1930s emphasized his dreamy, other-world qualities. In contrast, the 1940s Goofy (see opposite page) was a wilder, wackier creation.

With *Goofy and Wilbur,* Goofy emerged from the shadow of Mickey and Donald to take his place as a separate character with a life of his own. In *Goofy's Glider* (1940) and *How to Ride a Horse* (1941), Goofy consolidated his solo career. Yet from 1940 on, the world increasingly came to see a very different Goofy. He had become harder-edged, less dozy, with a much broader, rapid-fire comic style.

In addition, this new Goofy was practically voiceless. His "dialogue" was cut; he uttered only the laugh that was his trademark, the resigned "Gawrsh" with which he greeted the prospect of imminent catastrophe and, as this overcame him, a despairing "yeeeow!"

This radical break in style and approach must be explained. In fact, the more closely we look at the evidence, the more Goofy emerges as a confident, instinctive artist, responding to a changing climate inside and outside the Studio.

At the Disney Studio, the production of cartoon shorts was increasingly overshadowed by the full-length animated features of which the first was *Snow White and the Seven Dwarfs* (1937). To produce these features, Walt Disney developed a sophisticated, expensive approach to animation. It enabled Disney to create and sustain a complex mix of character, atmosphere, story-telling and emotion far beyond the demands of an 8-minute comedy short.

The rich, storybook quality of the Mickey, Donald and Goofy shorts from 1937 to 1939 was a spinoff benefit of the intense research into the technical and creative possibilities of animation in which the Studio was engaged at the time. But the level of effort devoted to shorts was the equivalent of putting an airplane engine into a Model T Ford. The Disney shorts, though universally acclaimed as the best in the field, were becoming too expensive to produce. A simpler, more economic approach was needed.

Meanwhile, a new comedy cartoon style was emanating from other animation studios. Realizing they could not achieve

the Disney quality, they concentrated on higher productivity and cost effectiveness. There was less emphasis on personality development and more on fast-paced slapstick comedy. In the forefront of the competing studios were Terrytoons, MGM, Paramount and Warner Brothers. The new stars were Daffy Duck (introduced in 1937), Tom and Jerry (1935), Woody Woodpecker (1940) and Bugs Bunny (1941).

The combination of financial constraint at the Disney Studio and changing comedy cartoon styles in general shaped Goofy's development in the 1940s. During that period, Goofy was to star in what were essentially formula cartoons. Just as Bugs Bunny was forever outwitting the slow-

Above and left: *How to Ride a Horse* (1941) confirmed Goofy's star appeal. Released as part of the live-action feature *The Reluctant Dragon* (1941), this cartoon showed director Jack Kinney's new-style Goofy playing against the off-screen narration of John McLeish. Kinney's team gave Goofy a broad, fast-paced comic style, in which the pompous voice-over of the narrator highlighted the total craziness of the action. In this sequence, Goofy attempts to demonstrate the use of spurs — but the horse decides it's one riding lesson he can do without!

thinking Elmer Fudd, and the unfortunate Tom was always in hot (and usually painful) pursuit of Jerry, so Goofy, too, followed a set pattern. And it was Disney director Jack Kinney, a big, brash, extroverted former newspaperman, who piloted Goofy into this hipper, slicker territory in the famous How-To series of cartoons.

Kinney was becoming impatient with the necessarily slower progress on the big features at Disney. He was only too eager to become involved in something that moved quickly, and in 1939 he got his opportunity. The Disney Studio set up individual production units for each character in the Disney menagerie, and Goofy was assigned to Kinney.

Jack Kinney had started with Disney in 1931, as an "inbetweener," one of the artists who painstakingly drew up the frame-by-frame sequences blocked out by animators. He was first hired by Disney in the early 1930s, and recalls: "I was given to know that the job might be just temporary. On October 23, 1957, when I was fired, I still believed it was only a temporary job!"

After a spell as an animator, Kinney was destined to move on to the Story Department. He eventually became a director on features and shorts.

In a quote from his memoirs, Kinney describes how the Goof came into his life in 1939:

"The Goofy series, luckily, came to me. From the Studio talent pool I drew a Class-A team — Ralph Wright, a keen story and gag man, and Jim Carmichael, who would handle story sketch along with Ralph and follow through into production layout. Lou Debney was my assistant director, and Woolie Reitherman and John Sibley were my lead animators.

"All told, we made up a competitive, on-the-bit and highly creative team that was perfect for turning out shorts of the kind I had planned for the Goofy series."

One of Kinney's major problems was that Goofy would not be able to talk very much. Pinto Colvig, who had provided Goofy's voice, had left the Studio in 1939 to join Max Fleischer's studio in Miami, so Goofy's dialogue would have to be dubbed from the sound tracks of past Goofy movies. Kinney's solution was to use a voice-over narration.

"We needed a voice that would be completely at variance with what was happening on the screen, the screwy situations that only Goofy could get into," he explained. "We wanted someone who could project a heavy, omniscient quality. Someone who talked it straight and pontifical, no matter what our gonged-out hero was doing!"

After many auditions of Hollywood's fanciest voice talents, the voice-over slot was still unfilled. Enter John McLeish, a Disney story sketch artist with more than a passing resemblance to the star John Barrymore and a voice to match. McLeish's resonant Shakespearian recitations were a regular entertainment in the Story Sketch Department.

Word got to Kinney about McLeish's talent, and an audition was rapidly arranged. Kinney recalls, "We tricked him into doing that thing. We gave him the dialogue and asked him to read it straight and serious. And he had the chance to really go all out with this great voice. He was on stage and just loved it. He was even giving us gestures!"

McLeish recorded several voice-over commentaries for Goofy before he found out what they were being used for. (He wasn't pleased when he did.) But the pompous, humorless narration worked. It provided a strong, but invisible, straight man for Goofy's silent, highly visual clowning — a new twist on the classic comedy act.

Here is Kinney's own account of how he devised the cost-effective formula that kept Goofy in business and in the public

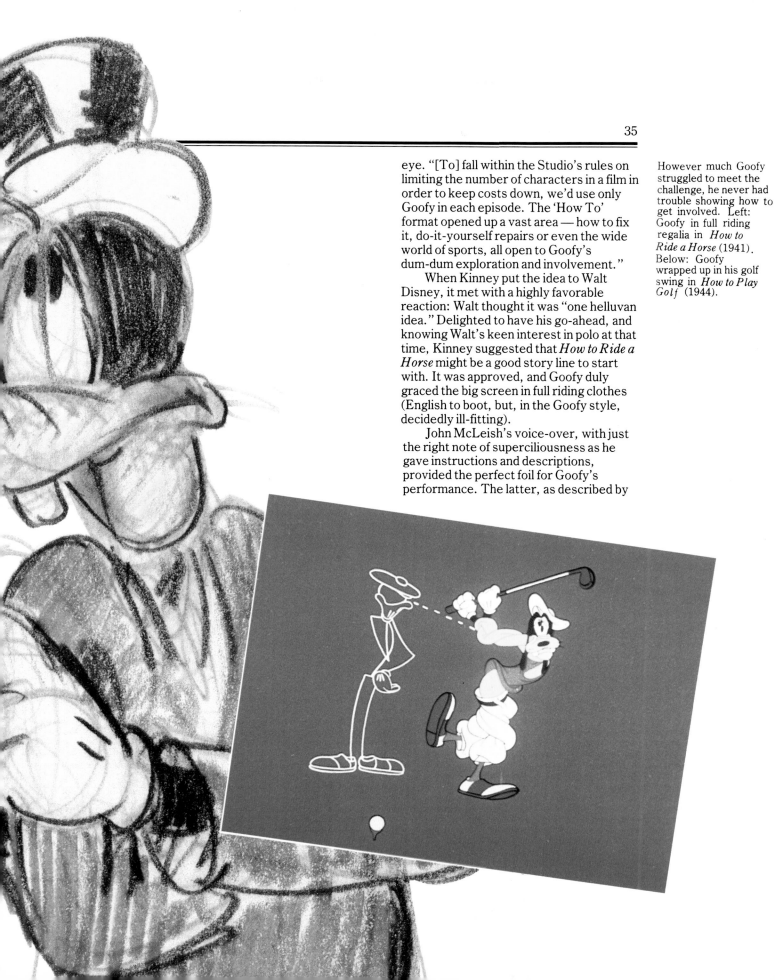

eye. "[To] fall within the Studio's rules on limiting the number of characters in a film in order to keep costs down, we'd use only Goofy in each episode. The 'How To' format opened up a vast area — how to fix it, do-it-yourself repairs or even the wide world of sports, all open to Goofy's dum-dum exploration and involvement."

When Kinney put the idea to Walt Disney, it met with a highly favorable reaction: Walt thought it was "one helluvan idea." Delighted to have his go-ahead, and knowing Walt's keen interest in polo at that time, Kinney suggested that *How to Ride a Horse* might be a good story line to start with. It was approved, and Goofy duly graced the big screen in full riding clothes (English to boot, but, in the Goofy style, decidedly ill-fitting).

John McLeish's voice-over, with just the right note of superciliousness as he gave instructions and descriptions, provided the perfect foil for Goofy's performance. The latter, as described by

However much Goofy struggled to meet the challenge, he never had trouble showing how to get involved. Left: Goofy in full riding regalia in *How to Ride a Horse* (1941). Below: Goofy wrapped up in his golf swing in *How to Play Golf* (1944).

Through the 1940s, Goofy forged a reputation for sporting klutziness on an epic scale. Right: Centerfield chaos in *How to Play Football* (1944). Below and bottom right: Goofy travels back 2,000 years to find sporting tradition roots in *The Olympic Champ* (1942). Top right: Goofoid basketball players tangle in *Double Dribble* (1946).

Kinney, was "the most ridiculous horsemanship seen since man first bestrode a shaggy prehistoric nag."

The "How-To" series was a winner from the start and provided as much fun for its creators as for the audiences who followed Goofy's "demonstrations" on the screen.

Jack Kinney, with the occasional story assistance of his brother Dick, went on to direct nearly all the Goofy shorts made between 1940 and 1953. In that time, Goofy brought his particular brand of sporting chaos to horse - back riding, gliding, skiing, boxing, baseball, the Olympic Games, swimming, fishing, golf, football, ice hockey, tennis, basketball, gymnastics and water skiing.

At one level, this unexpectedly athletic aspect of Goofy's wide-ranging enterprise reflected Jack Kinney's own sporting background as a junior high-jump champion

More golden moments from Goofy's sporting scrapbook. Right: *How to Swim* (1942). Below, left to right: *The Art of Self Defense* (1941) and *Goofy Gymnastics* (1949).

and later stalwart of the Disney Studio softball team. On another level, the series also marked an important development in Goofy's character as he mugged his way furiously through a host of sporting indignities. Decked by his own shadow in *The Art of Self Defense* (1941), trapped inside a chest expander in *Goofy Gymnastics* (1949), diving head first into a dry swimming pool in *How to Swim* (1942), he stands for every novice sportsman who has ever shanked a golf ball, racked up ten double faults in a row, been jumped on by a gorilla in a football outfit or had his best pitch knocked out of the ball park.

The gag sessions that led up to each new Goofy film were occasions of legendary hilarity. As Ollie Johnston and Frank Thomas recall, Goofy animators Woolie Reitherman and John Sibley were the chief instigators:

"The more they would talk, the funnier it would become to them, and soon they were just killing themselves laughing at all the gags. So they would decide to go and tell 'Ol' Kinney' about their new ideas, because he'd maybe think of something even funnier. Everyone could hear them going up and down the hall, talking and laughing about this with an occasional pause while one of them showed the other how it was going to be. Then the laughter would get even louder. By the time they were at Jack Kinney's room they were both in tears, but Jack knew the material so well he could pick right up with them and very soon was in convulsions, too."

Every comedy cartoon is a series of gags — from a sock on the jaw to a pie in the face — that keep the action cracking along. The Disney Studio had its quota of gag-men — ex-clowns like Pinto Colvig, former vaudeville comedians and so on — because cartoons *had* to be funny. What was always different about the Disney Studio was the attention paid to building up and pacing the action so gags would be funnier and also "right" for the personality of the character. Jack Kinney has this to say on the subject:

"Now these were all funny people, but they couldn't put a thing together. They were strictly gag-men — spot gags, sight gags and stuff like that. They couldn't do continuity or sequence material. The important thing was to tie the gags together with a theme and then to work out the timing against a prerecorded music score.

"Personality was important too: for example, Goofy is very easy going. In *Goofy's Glider* (1940), he takes a big fall out of the plane, maybe 250,000 feet. And he knows he has to count to 10 before he pulls the ripcord on his parachute. So we have him counting one… two… three and — kerboom — he hits the ground. It's too late. But he counts '10' and pulls the cord. That's the way he is — a slow thinker."

Jack Kinney and his team established Goofy with a new image and a formula for the 1940s. It was a long way from the barnyard hick of *Mickey's Revue* (1932), and different again from the slow-burning character brought to life by Art Babbitt. Goofy, as directed by Kinney, didn't think any faster than he had before — but he had acquired a sporting willingness to try anything once and an extra degree of physical energy to go with it.

Top and bottom left: *Goofy's Glider* (1940) was director Jack Kinney's first venture with Goofy and a foretaste of his sporting career to come. A fast-moving take-off soon provided Goofy with a new angle on his future.

Below: Duck-hunting Goofy collects a double-barrelled eyeful in *Foul Hunting* (1947).

Right: Goofy demonstrates nautical skills in *How to Be a Sailor* (1944). In this pocket history of seafaring through the ages, Goofy joined the U.S. Navy of World War II and, single-handedly, managed to destroy an entire enemy fleet.

Below: Pedal-powered Goofy encouraged wartime fuel-conservation in *Victory Vehicles* (1943).

Top far right: In *El Gaucho Goofy* (1943), Goofy clowned his way across the Argentinian pampas. The cartoon was part of a longer feature, *Saludos Amigos* (1943), designed to promote neighborly relations with South American countries whose continued neutrality was vital to wartime America.

In 1940, Disney moved from his crowded studios on Hyperion Avenue, Hollywood, to a modern, purposebuilt complex on a 53-acre site in Burbank, outside Los Angeles, in the San Fernando Valley. By then Walt had committed his organization to producing feature-length animated cartoons at a regular rate. But the onset of World War II brought disruption to the Studio.

At one point, a large part of the new studio was occupied by an entire unit of servicemen billeted on Disney at a moment's notice. Meantime, the government had requested Disney's help in producing a steady stream of top-priority instructional and informational animated films for the troops. And in 1941 the Studio was split by a bitter strike that resulted in the loss of some of its most creative people.

War meant the loss of Disney's European market and shortages of vital materials — everything from paper to color-film stock. Money was tight, too. Disney was spending to the limit and beyond on new features, such as the revolutionary *Fantasia* (1940), *Dumbo* (1941) and *Bambi* (1942).

The financial pressures meant *Bambi* (1942) was the last single-story, animated feature released by the Studio for 8 years. Production during the war years concentrated on short subjects. Between 1941 and 1945, the Studio released 77 cartoon shorts; Mickey Mouse starred in 5, Goofy 13, Pluto 17 and Donald Duck 36.

Three features were released between 1943 and 1945: *Victory Through Air Power* (1943), *Saludos Amigos* (1943) and *The Three Caballeros* (1945). But these were episodic productions, with short sections linked to a main theme.

Saludos Amigos grew out of Walt Disney's visit to Latin America in 1941 as a goodwill ambassador. With the world at war, it was vital for America to strengthen the links of friendship with her southern neighbors.

In a blend of live action and animation, the feature sparklingly evokes a Latin American atmosphere of carnival and exotic rhythms. Amid the fun, we find Goofy giving a typically off-the-wall demonstration of the legendary riding skills of the Argentinian gaucho, uncrowned king of the rolling pampas. Complete with a chaotic "slow-motion" sequence, this lighthearted parody had a serious purpose — to make American audiences aware of a rich South American tradition. Goofy's animated sequence was later released as a short, under the title *El Gaucho Goofy*.

With so much patriotic war work going on at the Studio, the Disney characters were also called upon to do their bit. Mickey, and especially Donald, made a number of screen appearances in uniform. Goofy's only front-line service was in the

U.S. Navy in *How to Be a Sailor* (1944). Here, however, he plays a heroic role as a humble member of the Pacific Fleet. In a typical Goofy gag, Goofy accidentally fires himself from a torpedo tube. But the mood of the film changes as Goofy surges through the waves to sink a whole fleet of enemy battleships, finally destroying a huge Rising Sun, the symbol of Japanese might. This is a stern and warlike Goofy — quite different from his normal easy-going self.

The year before, in *Victory Vehicles*, Goofy had made a more characteristic contribution to the war effort by showing how much gas could be saved if the entire population gave up their cars and exercised musclepower instead. The high spot of this film depicts Goofy in precarious charge of a pogo stick to the strains of the song, *Hop on Your Pogo Stick,* which became a popular hit. *Victory Vehicles* makes its serious point — that war involves people at home as well as at the battle front — with gentle humor and fantasy rather than strident patriotism.

One major contribution that Goofy — along with Mickey and Donald — made to morale during World War II was to appear on the insignia of many service units. Disney artists were kept busy designing such items as well working on wartime posters and instructional Government films, in which Goofy and many other Disney characters appeared.

Above: Disney characters were popular mascots and insignia for fighting men in World War II. Here, Goofy does his bit as the mascot for the 374th Two Engine Training Squadron.

GOOFY INTO THE POST-WAR PERIOD

GOOFY: FORTIES FAVORITE

Between 1941 and 1965, Goofy starred in 49 movies compared with Donald Duck's 106 and Mickey's 14. Undoubtedly, this makes Donald Duck the major Disney star of the era.

The unique vocal styling of the late Clarence "Ducky" Nash ensured that Donald was fully the raucous equal of Mel Blanc's gallery of Warner Brothers' cartoon crazies, including Bugs Bunny, Daffy Duck, Sylvester, Porky and the rest. And Donald was kept hard at work competing with them. Between 1941 and 1951, more than 450 cartoon shorts were produced by other studios — the equivalent of 4 feature-length movies a year.

So, while the prewar era at Disney came to be known as the Golden Age of Animation, the immediate postwar era of the cartoon cinema as a whole certainly deserves a special recognition for quantity production alone. Animators, such as Chuck Jones and Tex Avery, pushed the possibilities of the cartoon short to the limit and beyond, with increasingly wild action and crazy surrealist gags galore.

As we have seen, Jack Kinney was instrumental in taking Goofy into this new territory. Kinney was one of the four directors who piloted the Disney shorts through the 1940s. All four had risen through the ranks of the Disney organization. Jack King, Jack Hannah and Charles "Nick" Nichols completed the quartet. King and Hannah were responsible for Donald Duck, and Nichols partnered Mickey and Pluto.

A pool of writers — including Jack Kinney's brother Dick, Ralph Wright and Carl Barks of Donald fame — submitted ideas to the directors, who selected the stories they wanted. The director then chose four or five animators from the group assigned to short subjects to help him produce the film. It was common for one director to have up to six shorts at various stages of production at any one time.

If Donald was the Disney star of this period and Mickey — on screen at least — was a setting sun, Goofy was the accomplished genre performer. In the "How-To" films (see page 35), Goofy played a succession of sporting roles designed to please the 1940s taste for brash, fast, and often violent, cartoon comedy. Whatever disasters befell him, Goofy met them with stoic dignity, offering no more than a mute, reproachful look at the camera before meeting his doom.

Always trying to follow the narrator's instructions, Goofy flailed, momentarily triumphed, and fell. But somehow, the violence was diffused by Goofy's gentlemanly acceptance of it — what has been described as his "Olympian imperturbability" — and his unfailing readiness to try, try, try again.

By comparison, Donald appeared downright cantankerous while Bugs Bunny, Woody Woodpecker and other 1940s cartoon stars seemed almost psychotic in their aggression. Even so, the pace in Kinney's Goofy films could be fast and furious, as in *Hockey Homicide* (1945). In this film, a wild hockey game reaches a ferocious climax, exploding into

chaotic random images, including a shot of Monstro the Whale from *Pinocchio!*

In his authoritative history of the American animated film titled *Of Mice and Magic,* (1980), author Leonard Maltin points to *Hockey Homicide* (1945) as "reaching a peak of perfection" in closing the gap between the Disney approach and contemporary cartoon styles.

But Goofy's film activities in this period were not confined to the How-To sporting roles. A taste for travel and adventure took him to South America as a gaucho in *Saludos Amigos* (1943), to the Wild West as a fearless gunfighter in *Two Gun Goofy* (1952) and to Spain as a bullfighter in *For Whom the Bulls Toil* (1953).

He also went on two big-game hunting expeditions: to India in *Tiger Trouble* (1945) and to Africa in *Lion Down* (1951). In 1952, in a nostalgic look at Forties-style *film noir,* Goofy was even a private eye in *How to Be a Detective.*

Top left: *Hockey Homicide* (1945) remains the fastest, most furious of Goofy's 1940s sporting exploits. In the 1950s, he moved away from sport but still found time for other challenging roles. Here we see him (above) on the trail of an outlaw in *Two Gun Goofy* (1952), as world-weary private investigator Johnny Eyeball (center left) in *How to Be a Detective* (1952) and (below left) displaying devil-may-care daring as a matador in *For Whom the Bulls Toil* (1953).

Billposters (1940) was one of seven cartoons made between 1938 and 1950 in which Goofy and Donald Duck appeared without Mickey Mouse. Opposite and left: In this sequence, Goofy unknowingly pastes his poster on the revolving sails of a windmill and is surprised when the poster disappears. Below: An angry billy goat on his way to putting Goofy and Donald out of the bill-posting business! Directed by Clyde Geronimi, *Billposters* continued the story-book style of the classic 1930s shorts in contrast with the more boisterous antics of the How-To series.

Although the major part of Goofy's 1940s career was spent as a solo star, he made a number of appearances in his traditional role with the Disney stock company. *Billposters* (1940) depicts Goofy and Donald as paste-and-brush artists whose attempts to paste up advertising posters come unstuck somewhere between a windmill and a hungry goat.

The scenes alternate between the gentle Goofy and the aggressive Donald. Goofy, as the dreamy bumbler, absent-mindedly pastes his posters to the revolving sails of a windmill instead of the wall, touching off a slow spiral of mounting confusion. Meanwhile, the tasty tomato soup advertised on Donald's posters sharpens the appetite of a farmyard goat that starts to make a meal of the posters. Donald's rage is terrible, but the goat proves a formidable adversary, resulting in a battle royal.

The end of the film — and the end of our heroes' bill-posting career — finds Goofy and Donald marooned on the turning windmill after a severe drubbing at the hands, or rather the horns, of the vengeful billy goat.

Right: Faithful
crewmen Goofy and
Donald shape up in
Tugboat Mickey
(1940).

Tugboat Mickey (1940) is a rollicking
seafaring adventure in which Mickey,
Goofy and Donald take Mickey's tug to sea
in answer to a radio SOS from a ship in
distress. As stoker, Goofy does all he can
to respond to Mickey's call for "full steam
ahead" but runs into problems with the
tug's boiler.

When the furnace goes out, Goofy
goes inside to check out the trouble. The
furnace door slams shut, leaving Goofy in
the dark. With perfect logic Goofy strikes a
match to shed some light on the situation,
and the resulting explosion destroys the
boat completely. As the trio cling to the
wreckage, they discover that the "distress
call" was in fact only part of a radio play.

In *The Nifty Nineties* (1941) and
Orphan's Benefit (1941), Goofy makes only
brief appearances, but in *Mickey's Birthday
Party* (1942), Goofy plays the crucial role of
master chef. While the gang frolics in the

Left and below:
This typical Goofy gag —
from *Tugboat Mickey*
(1940) — shows Goofy
struggling with an
inanimate object. This
time, it's the door of
the ship's boiler that
gives our hero a
hard time.

Left and below: In *Mickey's Birthday Party* (1942), Goofy delivers a birthday surprise to Mickey in inimitable style.

living room, Goofy is destroying the kitchen in his attempts to bake Mickey's birthday cake.

In 1942, Goofy played the sousaphone in *Symphony Hour,* in which Mickey's radio orchestra struggles to please its irate sponsor Peg Leg Pete. When Goofy accidentally smashes all the orchestral instruments, things look black. But the orchestra's rendition of *Light Cavalry,* improvised on the remains of the instruments, turns out to be a wild success!

Between 1945 and 1947, Goofy starred in three shorts with Donald Duck. *No Sail* (1945) finds the pair all at sea and out of small change in a rented boat with a coin-operated motor.

Frank Duck Brings 'em Back Alive (1946) is a fast-paced spoof of the King Kong story, starring Goofy as the wild man of the tropical forest and Donald as the intrepid explorer determined to capture him. The result is best described as a bungle in the jungle.

The adventure theme is picked up again in *Crazy With the Heat* (1947), in which Goofy and Donald, stranded in the desert, are taunted with mirages of soda fountains, icebergs — and a polar bear.

Fun and Fancy Free (1947) was a full-length Disney animation feature with live-action introductions. One of the two cartoon episodes it contained was *Mickey and the Beanstalk,* a retelling of the classic folk tale. A high spot of the action has Goofy adrift in a gigantic pudding set on the giant's vast table. This episode marked the last joint screen appearance of the gang of three — Mickey, Goofy and Donald — until *Mickey's Christmas Carol* in 1983.

Below: Three mouseketeers step out as medieval peasants in *Mickey and the Beanstalk*, a featurette from *Fun and Fancy Free* (1947). This was the last screen appearance of Mickey, Goofy and Donald until the trio was reunited in *Mickey's Christmas Carol* (1983).

Goofy entered the 1950s as a new character — Mr. Geef. This average suburban man's losing struggles against rituals of suburban life form here a commentary on prosperous post-war America. Below: Mr. Geef is about to discover how hard it is to get away from it all in *Two Weeks Vacation* (1952). Center: It can be even more difficult to stay at home, however, as Mr. Geef discovered in *Father's Day Off* (1953).

The arrival of television in 1949 introduced new patterns of living and entertainment in America. The postwar generation was growing up in suburban homes with a television and hi-fi in the living room, electric appliances in the kitchen, and two cars in the driveway. All were signals of a home-based lifestyle of increasing comfort and prosperity.

Television was soon reflecting this lifestyle into the living room, with domestic comedy shows such as *I Love Lucy, The Burns and Allen Show* and *I Married Joan.* In 1954, the Disney Studio entered the new medium with a highly successful weekly show, *Disneyland,* and the following year with the *Mickey Mouse Club,* which was aired on the ABC network.

It was also in the 1950s that Goofy found yet another new role. From country bumpkin to solo Hollywood star (in the How-To series of zany sports spoofs made in the 1940s), Goofy had always sought to extend his range as a performer while retaining his comic personality as the amiable creator of chaos. Now, in the role of "Father" or sometimes Mr. Geef, the Goof portrayed the suburban anti-hero.

In more than a dozen films, Goofy teased out the comedy of Mr. Average Suburban Man, dealing incompetently with the ups and downs of modern life at home, at work and at play. Goofy was baffled by the art of photography in *Hold that Pose* (1950) and the logistics of taking a trip in *Two Weeks Vacation* (1952). *Father's Day Off* (1953) found him no better prepared for the demands of running a home and family in Mom's absence. Goofy continued to show that, even after years of experience, things still had a habit of getting on top of him.

These films of the 1950s have been criticized for taking the Goof *too* far from his roots. Yet it could be argued that they reflect exactly those changes taking place in society at the time.

In *Motor Mania* (1950), Goofy's portrayal of the Jekyll-and-Hyde Mr. Walker and Mr. Wheeler is, on one level, a gentle reminder that even the meekest character can become a power-crazed menace behind the wheel. But the demonic transformation of Goofy into the roadhog Mr. Wheeler is such a startling subversion of the familiar, lovable Goofy, that it makes us look for a deeper explanation.

Left and below: In *Motor Mania* (1950), the ultimate 1950s status symbol — the automobile — takes over. It transforms mild Goofy, as Mr. Walker, into the demonic Mr. Wheeler, terror of the highways. Playing against type casting, Goofy achieves new dramatic power in his portrayal of a modern Dr. Jekyll/Mr. Hyde.

Is it too much to suggest that, in his most mature phase as an artist, Goofy is hinting at a darker side of the American dream? If suburban man feels trapped in a conformist lifestyle, he may struggle comically in its grasp. But may he not also feel a destructive rage, an urge to break through the invisible barriers of inhibition?

Such thoughts suggest a bleaker aspect of Goofy's vision of the world than we are used to. Yet, we should not be afraid to look behind the apparent blandness of the 1950s Goofy in search of the complex artist we know him to be.

In *Father's Day Off* (1953), Goofy takes a trip deep into Jack Lemmon territory. Mom has taken a well-earned day out of the home, leaving Goofy to cope with Goofy Junior and the house. Under Goofy's gentle supervision, the routine crises of a housewife's day mount to a crescendo of domestic disorder. The competing demands of the phone, doorbell, child and family dog run poor Goofy ragged.

Consistent with the hint of suburban schizophrenia noted in *Motor Mania* (1950), the short *Father's Day Off* can be read in two ways. On the one hand, the incompetent Goof as the incompetent father is a natural piece of casting — the very stuff of 1950s comedy. From today's perspective, however, it can be seen as a subtle critique of conventional role-playing, suggesting the "natural" order of things demands that women stay at home while fathers go to work.

Social themes such as this offer a tantalizing glimpse of what Goofy might have gone on to do in this stage of his career if economic factors had not brought the era of cartoon films to a close.

In 1956, the Disney Studio finally stopped producing cartoon shorts on a regular basis. Television was stealing away former movie audiences, and the movie industry was responding with big-screen spectaculars. Three-hour-long Biblical epics, using gimmicks, such as 3-D, Cinemascope, Vistavision and stereophonic sound, were the order of the day. As theaters were refurbished and reconstructed, the old pattern of the evening picture show — newsreel, cartoon, second feature and main feature — began to disappear. And with Disney short cartoons now costing $75,000 each, there was no longer any money in theater distribution.

For three decades, Mickey, Minnie, Donald, Goofy and Pluto had been the standard-bearers of the Disney output of cartoon shorts, which averaged about 15 per year. But from 1955 to 1965, only 23 shorts were produced, of which Goofy made *Aquamania* (1961) which received an Academy Award nomination, *Freewayphobia* and *Goofy's Freeway*

Trouble, his last starring appearances, in 1965. The emphasis of the Studio had shifted to television and the resumption of full-length animated features which had been interrupted by World War II. Simultaneously, Walt Disney was realizing his dream project at Disneyland.

But if this period saw the end of Goofy's long and varied screen career, his character remained very much alive. In the Disney TV shows *Disneyland* and the *Mickey Mouse Club*, Goofy made a hit with the postwar generation. In comic strips and comic books, too, as well as on thousands of pieces of Disney merchandise, Goofy prospered as a much loved and instantly recognizable figure.

Goofy fills out his portrait of the common man, 1950s style. Top left: Goofy dreams of easy money in *Get Rich Quick* (1951). Far left: He worries about his health in *No Smoking* (1951). Below center and below: He discovers problems in running a home while Mom's away in *Father's Day Off* (1953).

GOOFY AND THE WORLD

GOOFY'S LIFESTYLE

Goofy's reality is one step beyond that of his friends Mickey and Donald. Even when he seems to be doing something simple, complications rapidly develop, in many instances due to his complete lack of coordination.

Animator Art Babbitt devised Goofy's highly individual walk (see page 19). And this remarkable, loose-limbed, almost balletlike response to a world of secret rhythms sabotages Goofy's every attempt to lead a normal life. In *How to Ride a Horse* (1941), one scene shows Goofy apparently riding his steed in a surprisingly competent, if rugged, style. A "slow motion" sequence that follows reveals the truth — Goofy is above, below, behind the horse — anywhere but on it. He is so uncoordinated that it takes a super-human degree of concentration on his part to appear merely clumsy.

But, as Henry Thoreau once pointed out, "If a man does not keep pace with his companions, perhaps it is because he hears a different drummer." And this makes Goofy a bit of a loner. Even Mickey, his best friend, can find Goofy's thinking a little baffling. Also, Goofy's well-meaning habit of undertaking any task in the most complicated manner possible has made his friends somewhat wary of asking him for help.

This sense of distance makes Goofy an elusive character to pin down, but it is all the more important that we do so. We will examine the "whole Goofy" in an attempt to sum up his off-screen lifestyle and personality.

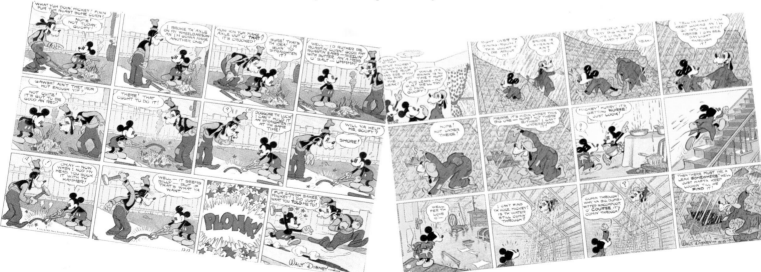

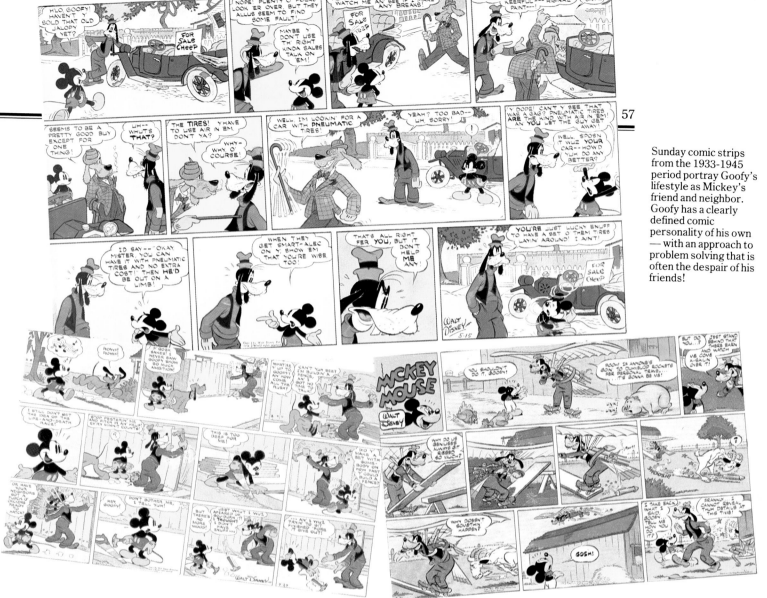

Sunday comic strips from the 1933-1945 period portray Goofy's lifestyle as Mickey's friend and neighbor. Goofy has a clearly defined comic personality of his own — with an approach to problem solving that is often the despair of his friends!

Elsewhere, we have concentrated on Goofy's art as evidenced through his performances on film in a wide range of roles. For an insight into Goofy's private life, the best evidence lies in the comic strips and comic books that have featured Goofy from 1933 to the present day. These are dealt with in detail on pages 80-87. Here we are concerned with the overall story.

The first aspect of Goofy's world to be dealt with is the full story of his relationship with Mickey and the inner circle of Disney characters. We've already seen that, in his original identity of Dippy Dawg, Goofy was the outsider of the gang — then made up of Mickey and Minnie Mouse, Horace Horsecollar and Clarabelle Cow. In the early days, Dippy was a crude, aimless, irritating fellow at times. He had a loud laugh, an aversion to hard work and an addiction to playing his "juice harp" at every opportunity, whether it was appropriate or not.

In plain language, Dippy was regarded as a pest with too thick a hide to know when he wasn't wanted. Yet within a year or two of this stage in his development (around

Below: Dippy Dawg to the rescue in the comic-strip adventure, *Mickey Mouse and the Terrible Bandit Wolf Barker* (1933). In this story, Dippy proved he was more than just a crude practical joker (bottom).

1932) he was on the way to becoming a valued friend. How did it happen? The turning point seems to have been in the newspaper comic-strip adventure *Mickey Mouse and the Terrible Bandit Wolf Barker*, published in early 1933.

The story starts as Dippy is left behind when Mickey and the gang go out West to take care of a ranch belonging to Mickey's Uncle Mortimer during his absence on business. Dippy wants to go too, but the general feeling is he'll be more of a hindrance than a help. Alternatively, it may have been the promise of several months in the company of Dippy's juice harp that swung the decision.

Certainly, when Dippy offers to give a hand with the baggage, he does nothing to improve his chances. He gives the baggage to a junkman mistaking him for the delivery man, then disappears at the train station when asked to watch the trunks. And why

has a pile of Clarabelle's clothes been left on the station platform? The question is soon answered — Dippy has stowed away inside Clarabelle's cabin trunk aboard the train.

The sound of a twanging juice harp inside the trunk tells us where Dippy is but scares the baggage attendant. Convinced the trunk is haunted, he throws it off the train. Dippy kicks holes in the trunk for his legs and — in a mood to take things as they come — hikes off across the prairie.

Meanwhile, Mickey and friends have transferred to a stagecoach for the journey from the station to Uncle Mortimer's spread. On a lonely stretch of trail, the stagecoach is ambushed at gunpoint by the gold-hungry villain, Wolf Barker, and his sidekick.

An already-tense situation becomes even more desperate when Wolf decides to abduct the spirited Minnie. But — at this moment of almost unbearable danger — enter a walking, twanging cabin trunk! Terrified by this surrealistic apparition, the bandits flee empty-handed, and Dippy is hailed as the hero of the day.

This episode marks an important revaluation of Dippy's character in preparation for his initiation into Mickey's club. His aimlessness is, at a stroke, reinterpreted as a goodnatured, easy-come-easy-go approach. His "dippiness" is shown to be less foolishness and more of a freewheeling approach to solving problems.

In this light, there is no longer anything barring Dippy's entry into the camaraderie of the group. From now on, he is a new element in the mix — the gentle anarchist who creates new possibilities and surprises simply by being himself.

At the time when Dippy/Goofy first joined the gang, Mickey, Minnie, Horace and Clarabelle were completing their move from the barnyard to small-town respectability. The mischievous Mickey of 1928 to 1931 was a talking rodent whose humor could be wild and even cruel. He was only one step less of an animal than the horses, cows, dogs and pigs around him.

By 1932, however, Mickey was a star, and people wanted to know more about him. Parents and community leaders wanted to be satisfied that he was a good influence. So Mickey changed his rodent image to that of a high-spirited, adventurous all-American boy. Of course, a hero has to have friends, so some of Mickey's barnyard companions were selected to become more human along with Mickey.

Minnie was obviously Mickey's girlfriend; Horace and Clarabelle were their slightly older friends. By the same token, Dippy/Goofy, and later, Donald Duck, can be seen as recruits promoted from the ranks of barnyard characters to "human" status. And if Dippy/Goofy still retains an element of the rural anarchy of those days, so Donald's aggression harks back to the slam-bang humor of the early Mickey Mouse films.

In the newspaper comic strips of 1933

Left: Dippy threatens a promising career as a detective by stealing the mayor's car in the comic-strip story, *Mickey Mouse the Detective* (1933–4).

From shiftless Dippy to comrade-in-arms, Goofy's life became more closely linked to the adventurous career of Mickey. Typical scenes from (left to right) *Mickey Mouse the Detective* (1933–34), *Mickey Mouse on Cave Man Island* (1940–41), *Mickey Mouse and the Dude Ranch Bandit* (1940) and *Mickey Mouse and the Black Crow Mystery* (1942).

to 1934, Dippy was established as a friend and neighbor of Mickey in the small-town setting that was to be their home for many years. By 1936, in the comic-strip adventure, *Mickey Mouse and the Great Ostrich Race*, Dippy had become Goofy, a nickname with greater overtones of affection than Dippy.

Newly furnished with a more human physique, Goofy was now free to develop in his own way. Swedish Goofy-expert Horst Schroeder has described Goofy's social identity at this time as "the well-meaning fool who always fails to follow the social norms and who, as a consequence, becomes the butt of the jokes of the better-adjusted." But, as Schroeder also points out, Goofy is less of a fool than he looks, more a screwball thinker who "knows what he wants even though the world around him believes that he should have known better."

Meanwhile, Goofy's friendship with Mickey and newcomer Donald became the basis of professional collaboration as fellow performers. For many individuals, the bonds of friendship may be tested to breaking point by such an experience — but Goofy appears to have coped well.

Goofy's good nature seems to have been the strength that was fully equal to the demands of both a burgeoning screen career and the need to live in relaxed harmony with his friends. For example, his relationship with Horace and Clarabelle never suffered from the fact that, at a time when Goofy was becoming a leading Disney screen player, Horace and Clarabelle were making fewer screen appearances.

This good nature — and the left-field quality of Goofy's mind — allowed him to develop the independence that underpins his career as a solo star. During the mid-1930s, however, Goofy was still

establishing the lifestyle that has continued, albeit with some variations, until today.

One mystery that may never be solved is the question of how Goofy earned a living during these years — unless income from his screen appearances was enough to cover his needs. He always seemed to have a lot of time on his hands — to go fishing, to lie in his hammock or to join in Mickey's comic-strip adventures. The latter provided Goofy with a rich store of experiences — richer by far than the original Dippy could ever have dreamed of.

As Mickey's loyal — if occasionally bungling — comic-strip companion, he took two trips to the Wild West, in *Mickey Mouse and the Terrible Bandit Wolf Barker* (1933) and in *Mickey Mouse and the Dude Ranch Bandit* (1940). He also traveled to the mysterious East in *Mickey Mouse and the Sacred Jewel* (1934). He worked as a detective in *Mickey Mouse the Detective* (1933-34) and as a ghost-hunting sleuth in *Mickey Mouse and the Seven Ghosts* (1936).

He shipped out with Mickey on a whale-hunting expedition in *Mickey Mouse, Mighty Whalehunter* (1938), explored a lost prehistoric world in *Mickey Mouse on Cave Man Island* (1940-41) and volunteered for war work on the land in *Mickey Mouse and the Black Crow Mystery* (1942). His role in these adventures is generally that of Dr. Watson to Mickey's go-getting role of Sherlock Holmes. Goofy accepted Mickey's leadership ability, but he was often able to come up with an unexpected twist of his own.

Over the years, Goofy has lived in a variety of houses, from crazy wood shacks to modern suburban homes. Indeed, in the comic strips and comic books of the 1940s and 1950s, the home town of Mickey and Goofy seems to have become increasingly suburbanized. But as a private individual, Goofy never seems to have lived the comfortable family life he portrayed on the screen in the 1950s. At heart, he is not the domestic type, and is perhaps something of a loner. Even so, by the end of the 1950s he seems to have settled into a quieter way of life — without losing any of his originality as a thinker.

Indeed, Goofy's highly individual approach extends to every facet of his life. Some aspects are described in the following pages where we take a look at his extensive wardrobe, and at his success (or otherwise) with the ladies.

Unlike Mickey and Donald, Goofy always dressed for the part, wearing many outfits through the years. But he always had problems getting them to fit!

It is interesting to note that while it was a long time before Mickey had a shirt and Donald *never* had a pair of trousers, Goofy was given a complete suit of clothes early in life. His outfit of hat, sweater, vest, long pants and oversize shoes was, frankly, sloppy. The pants were often patched. The shoes usually needed repair, and the hat was battered. Even so, sensitive Goofy-watchers claim to have noticed that behind Goofy's casual-dress sense lurked a secret obsession with clothing and fashion.

Goofy has appeared in many different outfits during his long career. In the comic strip adventure *Mickey Mouse and the Seven Ghosts* (1936), Goofy suddenly acquires a deerstalker hat and meerschaum pipe à la Sherlock Holmes. At the end of the adventure, Goofy buys a new suit with some of the reward money he receives for his part in capturing a gang of criminals.

The suit is three sizes too large, with a brutally loud check, but Goofy loves every square inch of it.

In another comic-strip story, *Mickey Mouse and the Dude Ranch Bandit* (1940), Goofy decks himself out in 10-gallon hat, gunbelt, sheepskin chaps and high-heeled boots as the complete Hollywood-style singing cowboy.

On the screen, the long sequence of movies that begins with *How to Ride a Horse* (1941), presents Goofy in a wide variety of sporting attire.

Given the weight of evidence, then, can we say that Goofy is really something of a dandy? Or, as some have suggested, should we see the constant changes of costume as a sign of a deep-seated identity crisis? The answer to both questions is surely a resounding "No!" Goofy's extensive wardrobe is simply part of his all-over "Goofiness." He dresses the part, in clothes always too big or too small, to remind us that he is a clown, and to signal that whatever he is about to do will be richly, hilariously absurd.

Goofy's mode of dress could also be a highly successful attempt on his part to keep our attention, even when he is in one of his supporting roles, rather than a starring one. Certainly it isn't easy to overlook him!

Goofy's romantic adventures have been ill-starred, but his native gallantry remains noble to the end. Here he falls for a couple of real dolls in (below) *Clock Cleaners* (1937) and (opposite) *Boat Builders* (1938).

What of romance in Goofy's life? As with so much in Goofy's world, this is also something of a mystery. Both Mickey and Donald have had long-standing, well-publicized relationships. Mickey has been linked with the spirited and loyal Minnie, Donald with the mercurial Daisy. Both couples have survived the stresses and strains of life in the public eye.

Goofy, however, has never had his name linked romantically with anyone — perhaps because of an intense bashfulness in the presence of the opposite sex. This is sad because Goofy is a deeply romantic figure, capable of the noblest affections. Two comic–tragic episodes illustrate this aspect of his personality.

In *Clock Cleaners* (1937), Goofy is confronted with the stately figure of Liberty, one of the two automata (the other is Father Time) who strike the hours on a great clock. Instantly Goofy is covered in confusion, stammering "Gawrsh, a lady," as the automaton, wielding a fearsome mallet, advances toward him. Rooted to the spot, Goofy struggles for words, only to receive a heavy whack to the head. A dazed Goofy walks off the belltower parapet, beginning an aerial walkabout that can be viewed as a superb exercise in clowning or a romantic ecstasy.

In the second episode, from *Boat Builders* (1938), Goofy falls in love with a ship's figurehead — a pert and buxom beauty — whom he imagines to be a "living doll". The figurehead, carried by Mickey, appears to play a roguish game of peek-a-boo with the smitten Goofy. With eyes tight shut, Goofy plants a smacking kiss — on the ship's hooter, which lets out a piercing whistle. With a cry of "Whattagirl!" Goofy rises rapturously into the air.

These sentimental pas de deux, tinged as they are with melancholy, are the earliest clues to Goofy's romantic life. Much later on, as Mr. Geef, the suburban hero of the 1950s films, Goofy is seen with a wife and child. But whether he ever did overcome his bashfulness sufficiently to get married is an open question. Such an action would seem out of character, and we should probably see Mr. Geef as a role played by Goofy, the actor, rather than a true reflection of his real-life circumstances.

BRINGING GOOFY TO LIFE

ANIMATING GOOFY

MOUTHFULL

Disney characters, like Goofy, Donald Duck and Mickey Mouse, have become so much a part of our lives that it is easy to think of them as real people rather than two-dimensional images of ink and paint. In this book we have talked about Goofy as though he were a live actor — but now it is time to look inside the Disney Studio and find out about the actual processes that were used to bring Goofy to life.

In 1932, when Goofy made his first screen appearance in *Mickey's Revue*, the Disney Studio was housed in a cramped, old building on Hyperion Avenue in Hollywood. Walt Disney was the young, successful leader of the most famous animation studio in the world. In Mickey — whose fourth birthday fell that year — Disney had a movie personality "with a bigger screen following than nine tenths of the stars in Hollywood," according to columnist Louella Parsons.

Yet Mickey — and all the other Disney characters that followed him — began life as drawings on pieces of paper. Thousands of drawings had to be made before even one 8-minute cartoon could be produced.

The animated cartoon is a highly specialized form of cinema. A live action movie camera breaks down movement into a series of still pictures or frames — 24 per second at normal speed. Each frame is a snapshot of a piece of movement a little different from the one that went before. The trick lies in something called "persistence of vision." The human eye retains the image of what it sees for about $\frac{1}{10}$ second. If enough still images quickly pass before the human eye, each in a slightly different position, they will create the appearance of continuous movement.

The creator of an animated film exploits this illusion to imitate movement. If he wants to make a cartoon character move its arm, he draws a number of pictures of the arm in the various stages of movement. Each drawing is photographed by a static cine camera, one frame at a time, and when the film is projected — the arm will appear to move!

Before 1928 animated films were silent, and so depended on visual humor to give the characters life and appeal. Then Walt Disney introduced synchronized sound, and the animated figures could suddenly speak, play musical instruments or do funny actions in time with a musical background score. The effect was magical.

The secret of Disney's success was the hard work and meticulous preparation his team put in to synchronize the visual action with the sound track. Each 8-minute cartoon was packed with enough gags — bits of comic "business" — to keep a step or three ahead of the first-time viewer.

The organizational genius of Walt Disney broke down the elements of sound track, visuals and comedy into the main stages that, in sequence, made up the finished cartoon. These stages were *story, score* (or sound track), *background, animation, finished drawing, inking and painting* and *camera.* Over the years, each

HAIRS FOLLOW BROW DOWN IN A FROWN

HAT FITS OVER TOPNOT

CROTCH STRETCHES

...NOUT TURN UP IN A SMILE & THE CORNERS OF THE MOUTH SHOW—SNOUT DROOPS DOWN IN ANGER

EVERY COSTUME THE GOOF WEARS IS LOOSE FITTING & HAS A LOW CROTCH

BIG...
WH...

Far left: Walt Disney, in the mid-1930s, was the founder and leader of the most famous animation studio in the world.

Left: 1937 Studio model sheet shows how Disney artists communicated Goofy's personality through facial expression, posture and costume.

stage was to become even more refined and complex as Disney expanded his team. Tasks that were originally handled by one or two individuals needed entire departments to see them through.

We have seen how animator Art Babbitt — Goofy's "fairy godfather" — joined Walt Disney's team at a time of expansion (see page 15). So let's look at how a Disney cartoon was produced in 1934, when the products of the Disney Studio had already established themselves as being far ahead of the competition.

A Goofy cartoon began with the *storyboard*. This was a Disney invention, credited to Webb Smith. The storyboard was a series of drawings that told in pictures the complete story of the cartoon from the opening shot to the last shot. The artists in the Story Department prepared these drawings and pinned them up in sequence on a 4×8ft (1.2×2.4m) board (hence storyboard).

One of the artists then presented the sequence to Walt Disney in a meeting in which the story was mercilessly criticized. It was tough for the presenter, but the meeting was an opportunity to cut out weak material and tighten up the story line. In an 8-minute cartoon there wasn't time for slack or dull moments when the viewer might lose interest. In storyboard sessions, Walt was a rich source of ideas for keeping the action moving.

It usually took several storyboard sessions before the final version was agreed upon. Then, the story was handed over to the director, who was responsible for seeing the entire film through, from storyboard to final print.

From the storyboard, the director constructed an *exposure sheet*, another Disney invention. This divided the 8-minute film into the necessary number of frames. The story was then plotted out over the number of frames, according to the amount of time allotted to each

episode within the story.

The first stage of actual production was to record the soundtrack of the entire 8-minute film. Through experience, the Studio had found that this was the best way to achieve the perfect synchronization of sound and pictures for which Disney had become famous. Working from the final storyboard and the exposure sheets the director made up a bar chart. This plotted music, dialogue, sound effects and visuals against the frame-by-frame progress of the action to be animated.

The bar chart — one more Disney invention — was like a conductor's score. It allowed everyone who worked on the picture to see just what would be happening at any point, to within 1 foot (16 frames) of film. A system of musical beats (one every six frames) and accents told the musician the tempo and indicated where he might need to vary it or add a particular effect. With the bar sheet as reference, music, dialogue and sound effects were recorded on separate tracks.

When the crucially important music sound track was complete, it had the precision of the finest Swiss watch. Only then did the process of animation begin — bringing to life the sequence of drawings so carefully worked out on the storyboard.

At this point, the director gave his bar chart to the animator. As one might expect, the animator is at the heart of the animated film. He designs the action that occupies the sequence of footage. Perhaps the best definition of the animator's job is that he is "an actor with a pencil." Just like an actor, he is in control of a character — in this case, Goofy.

The animator has to know his character inside out and make the character perform the action in an entertaining fashion to fit a prerecorded musical sound track. Originally, the animator sketched every frame of the action: the character would move its feet,

its hands and its body frame by frame. As each frame was sketched on a separate piece of paper, animators worked with several sheets pegged together, stopping every few seconds to roll or flip the sheets to see if the action "flowed."

In the Disney Studio, however, it became the rule that animators did not necessarily draw every stage in a character's action sequence. In the interests of speed, Disney decided the animator needed only to sketch the "extremes" — the exaggerated positions between which the character would move.

Another artist, who was known as an "inbetweener," worked out all the intermediate poses and drew them in. At this stage, the whole sequence — rough as it was — would be filmed to give the animation team an idea of how things were going.

In the crowded Hyperion Avenue Studio, a tiny room was kept clear for Walt Disney to view these rough working prints. This room was soon known as "the sweatbox," and as time went on, the process of viewing the working prints came to be called "sweatboxing." Disney himself was a perfectionist, and it sometimes took many sweatbox sessions before he was prepared to approve a sequence.

Walt Disney's unremitting drive to improve the quality of his Studio's cartoons produced a very special style of animation. Disney wanted movement to flow, but more than that he wanted action and characters that audiences could respond to emotionally. The artists in the Studio studied how posture, mannerism, movement and gesture could express character or emotion.

Don Graham, an art teacher from the Chouinard Art School in Los Angeles gave the artists lessons in life drawing. Evening sessions were first held in Art Babbitt's house and later at the Studio.

Below left: Pinto Colvig, musician, gag man and former clown, was Goofy's voice.

Below: Walt Disney and musicians — including Pinto Colvig on clarinet — work out a score for a new cartoon around 1938. Recording the sound track first helped directors to get a perfect mesh of sound and action.

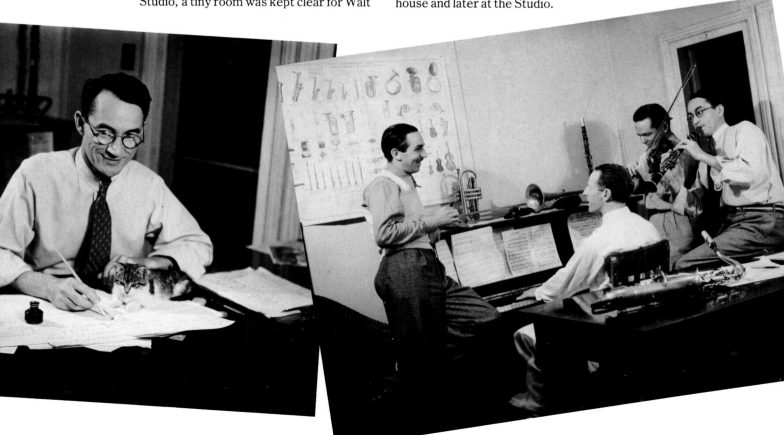

Don Graham taught anatomical drawing and took the artists on field trips to the zoo and into the countryside to study the movement of birds and animals. Animators also studied live-action movies — from Chaplin comedies to the work of the most avant-garde European directors — for sequences or tricks that might be adapted to improve animation.

In the course of this constant research and practice, the Studio evolved certain rules and principles of animation. Three of the most important principles were Anticipation, Squash-and-Stretch and Overlapping Action.

Disney was a great fan of vaudeville and silent comedy and he knew that what made an action funny was *exaggeration*, the *set-up* (when a character notices something), *pointing* (exaggerating the action which follows) and the *follow-through* (the little actions that continue after the main action is complete). So

Anticipation meant having the character prepare the audience for the next movement. The set-up could be a small action, such as a glance, or a broad action, as when a character draws back before rushing out of the scene.

Squash-and-Stretch was an important element in Disney animation. When Goofy is whacked on the head in *Clock Cleaners* (1937), his whole head and body squashes up. But when he is teetering on the parapet of the clock tower, his body becomes stretched out.

Disney artists came to treat their cartoon figures as having a "volume" that had to be maintained consistently in any pose. They practiced by drawing a half-filled flour sack in squashed, stretched and twisted positions to study how this might be achieved. They even drew the sack in poses expressing emotion, exploring how the Squash-and-Stretch principle could convey character and attitude.

Right: Draft script for *Clock Cleaners* (1937). The action, described scene by scene, was carefully worked out to fit a prerecorded sound track.

Overlapping Action, or "follow-through," kept up the expressiveness of the action, even after it was completed. If a character came to a complete stop, there was a break in the flow. If Goofy is walking along and something catches his eye, his head turns — but his body keeps going forward for a second or two before turning to catch up with his head. As a further refinement, different parts of Goofy's body move at different speeds, conveying the uncoordinated and aimless aspects of his personality.

The effect of these techniques and their refinements was to give Disney animation its distinctively liquid, flowing and weighty quality. A highly flexible control over relatively small adjustments in movement also helped to build personality into a character.

In Art Babbitt's animation, Goofy's movements are a loose-limbed shuffle. His eyes are half shut and respond slowly to what they see, suggesting a certain dreaminess. Goofy tends to look long and hard at the things he does notice, conveying a slow pace of thought.

In Woolie Reitherman's animation, on the other hand, Goofy is less of a dreamer and more of an exuberant klutz. His arms and legs windmill wildly, and his long, resigned stare into the camera is not so much stupidity as a plea for sympathy.

Resuming the discussion of the sequence in which cartoon films were made: once the animation sequences were approved, it was time to "clean-up," or finalize, all the drawings. At this point, all the drawings were still on paper. The next step was to trace the outlines onto transparent celluloid sheets, known as *cels*, that were placed over the drawings. This was done before the cels were turned over to the artists who applied color to the back side of the cel. More than 2,000 different tints were kept in the Disney color laboratory.

Meanwhile, from the beginning of production, background and layout artists were preparing the backgrounds against which the characters would appear. In the Disney Studio, backgrounds were elaborately and beautifully painted.

In the final stage of production, the cels were laid over the backgrounds and photographed frame by frame by a cine camera. With many cels laid on top of one another in any shot, this was a time-consuming task. When the first print of the cartoon was ready, it was matched up with its prerecorded sound track.

If the process of production sounds complicated — it was! Disney's search for perfection in every department of production — Story, Music, Animation, Layout and Background, Inking and Painting — made his cartoons very

expensive to produce. In 1935, an 8-minute cartoon cost around $35,000. The economics of the business meant it took the Studio 18 months to get its money back on the project.

With more people becoming involved at every stage of production, the Studio followed a policy of not crediting individual artists on the grounds that the complex production process was an integrated team effort. Today, the interest in the history of Disney animation art over the last half century is so great that the names of individual artists and animators have become well-known among serious Disney fans. Men like Ub Iwerks, Hamilton Luske and Norman Ferguson from 1928-32; Art Babbitt, Bill Tytla, Fred Moore in the 1933-40 period and Ward Kimball, Frank Thomas, Ollie Johnston, Woolie

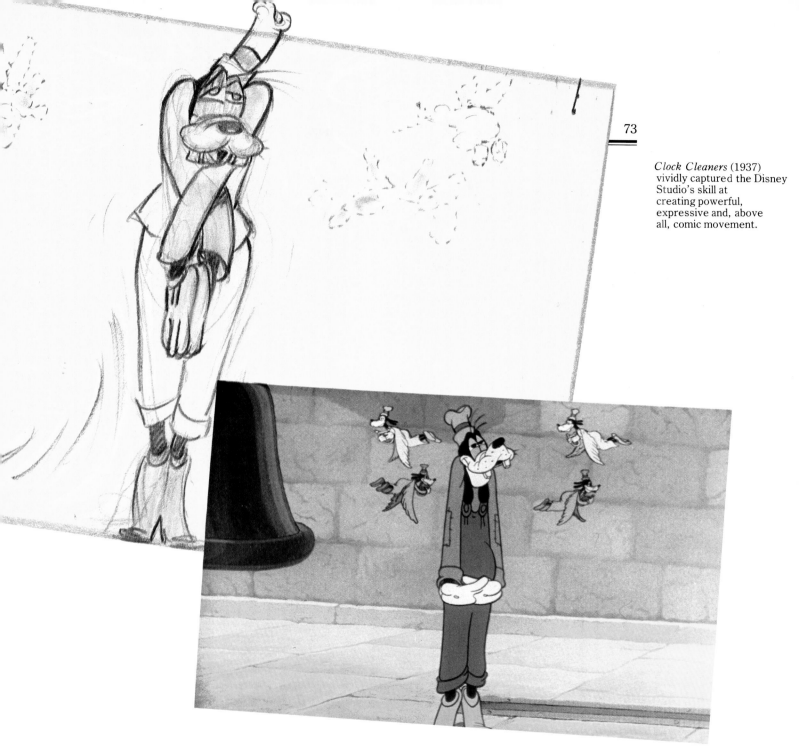

Clock Cleaners (1937) vividly captured the Disney Studio's skill at creating powerful, expressive and, above all, comic movement.

Reitherman and Milt Kahl from the late 1930s onward.

Under Disney's leadership, these men took animation from the scampering, rubbery barnyard figures of the early days at Disney to the rich, colorful, expressive images of full-length features such as *Snow White and the Seven Dwarfs* (1937), *Pinocchio* (1940), *Fantasia* (1940) and *Bambi* (1942).

The two figures who were most influential in bringing Goofy to life were Art Babbitt and Woolie (short for Wolfgang) Reitherman. As described on page 16, Babbitt developed the character from a "barnyard schnook," as he puts it, into a fully animated personality.

Says Babbitt, "the character gave me a chance to try out all sorts of animation tricks that hadn't been tried before — things that cannot happen in real life, and yet they're perfectly acceptable in animation."

Two of the Babbitt touches were the Goofy flip-flop walk and shuffling body movements, both finely displayed in the three Mickey, Donald and Goofy pictures he worked on: *Mickey's Service Station* (1935), *On Ice* (1935) and *Moving Day* (1936).

After completing these three shorts, Babbitt worked on full-length features. He animated the Wicked Queen in *Snow White and the Seven Dwarfs* (1937) and the dancing mushrooms in *Fantasia* (1940).

Meanwhile, the Babbitt-designed Goofy continued in the Mickey, Donald and Goofy series of shorts: *Moose Hunters* (1937), *Hawaiian Holiday* (1937), *Clock Cleaners* (1937), *Lonesome Ghosts* (1937), *Boat Builders* (1938), *Mickey's Trailer* (1938), *The Whalers* (1938) and *Tugboat Mickey* (1940). In these pictures, the trio appeared together at the start of the film, split up for individual sequences and reassembled for the finish.

Woolie Reitherman, the long-serving Disney animator, film and TV director, took over Goofy as a member of Jack Kinney's production unit on *Goofy's Glider* (1940) and *How to Ride a Horse* (1941). Famous for his boundless energy and enthusiasm for squeezing the last ounce of entertainment value from his animation, Reitherman also worked on two of the most powerful sequences in Disney features. These were Monstro the Whale

in *Pinocchio* (1940) and the dinosaurs of *Fantasia* (1940).

In their book *Disney Animation: The Illusion of Life*, published in 1981, authors Frank Thomas and Ollie Johnston offer their verdict on Reitherman's work with Kinney on the Goofy films:

"The Goofy that Woolie animated communicated with the audience in a way that only Woolie could have done it — this was a new type of animation."

More recently, in conversation, Frank Thomas expanded his judgment: "Woolie's Goofy is less dreamy than Art's. He's still none too bright and accident-prone, but he's more no-holds-barred and gung-ho."

Reitherman's own assessment of his approach is: "My work had vitality and an 'I don't give a damn, try it' quality."

This broader approach is evident in the sports roles assumed by Goofy in the Kinney-Reitherman How-To series. The sports theme allowed for a greater wealth of slam-bang physical gags than Goofy encountered in the Mickey, Donald and Goofy series.

In the hands of Woolie Reitherman, solo star Goofy was able to develop into a jack-of-all-trades whose incompetence is matched only by his enthusiasm.

Left: Goofy director Jack Kinney (right) with Walt Disney (center) and story artist Lance Nolley working on *Fun and Fancy Free* (1947).

Below left: Wolfgang (Woolie) Reitherman, lead animator on Jack Kinney's Goofy team.

GOOFY FOR SALE

MERCHANDISING GOOFY

In 1930, Walt Disney and his brother Roy made the decision to merchandise Disney characters on a fully commercial basis. The first contract letter, dated Feb. 3, 1930, confirms the granting of sole rights to Geo. Borgfeldt & Co. to manufacture "Figures and Toys of various materials, embodying your design of comic Mice known as MINNIE & MICKEY MOUSE."

By 1935, with the help of Kansas City promotion man Herman "Kay" Kamen, Disney-character merchandise was doing $35 million a year in retail sales.

With the enthusiastic backing of Walt and Roy Disney, Kamen rapidly built up a solid merchandising organization to maximize the efficiency with which Disney licenses were granted. At the same time, the Disneys retained full control over the quality of the merchandise licensed.

One department at Disney dealt with legal and technical issues of licensing agreements. Another coordinated Mickey Mouse promotions in the retail store trade. An advertising agency was commissioned to design packaging, products and promotional material.

By mid-1948, due to Kamen's efforts, more than 2,000 articles of Disney character merchandise were being produced and distributed by 150 companies in the United States and 500 throughout the rest of the world.

The impact of Mickey Mouse's merchandising magic has been analyzed by Cecil Munsey in his book *Disneyana: Walt*

Below: Painted plaster model of Goofy, dating from late 1930s. This is one of many models made in the Disney Studio to help animators visualize characters.

Center: Novelty playing cards feature "The Goof" in his early form.

Far right: Beginning of Disney merchandising — Walt Disney and staff with Mickey Mouse dolls in February 1930.

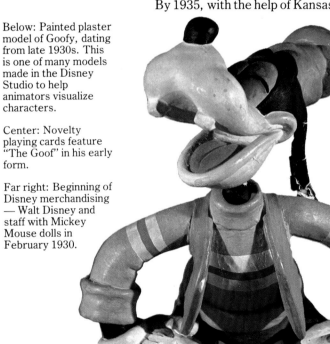

Disney Collectibles, published in 1974. The book lists over 100 items or categories of items highly sought-after by collectors, and summarizes matters thus:

" … Mickey Mouse was the best-known and most popular figure of the day. In the area of character merchandising, whatever Mickey endorsed sold, and in most cases, sold very well."

Here, "very well," meant "in millions." A single item illustrates this point. In 1933, the Ingersoll-Waterbury Company received a license to manufacture Disney-character clocks and watches. In 1948, Kay Kamen was able to present Walt Disney with the 5-millionth Mickey Mouse watch. Nine years later, Disney received the 25-millionth Mickey watch!

As Disney merchandise continued its phenomenal success, Goofy, also, came to be seen on a wide range of objects from 1935. In the early merchandising days — the 1930s — he appeared as Dippy Dawg and was most often to be found in the background. On a decorative tin of the period, for instance, Dippy might be seen in the background of a painted picnic scene involving the other cartoon characters. But even then, he was present as one of the gang.

The equation of Mickey as leader and initiator of new adventures and Donald with his customary bluster and aggression, plus Dippy/Goofy as left-field loony, had come to be associated with an inexhaustible fund of entertainment. Just the sight of any one, or all three, of the famous trio brought smiles to the faces of millions.

Because this is Goofy's biography, all the merchandise shown on these pages features him, although — as mentioned before — in the 1930s and into the 1940s, he was not usually featured solo. More recently sculptor Blaine Gibson has produced a limited-edition Goofy sculpture, which has been acclaimed as one of the more desirable Disney artifacts.

Today, as Sport Goofy (see page 90 for details) the Goof is rapidly becoming established as a major merchandising character in his own right. Already, he has been seen in over 30 different sporting outfits. In addition, his cheerful, ear-to-ear grin and wacky antics decorate a wide range of Adidas sporting accessories — impressive evidence of Goofy's new status in the sports world and of his great popularity and selling power.

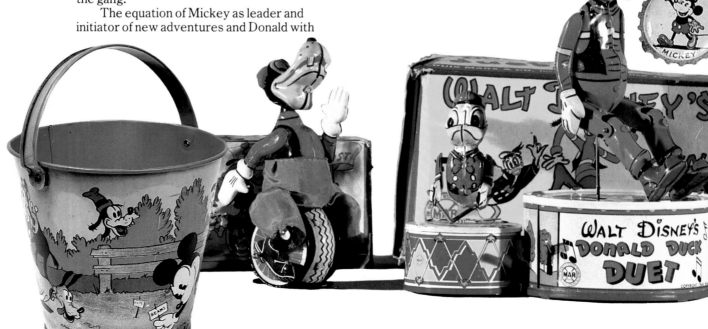

The first Disney publication, the *Mickey Mouse Book* (1930), was published in New York by Bibo and Lang. Today, the international production of Disney books is a significant sector of the publishing industry. At the last count, over 180 publishers worldwide, are licensed to produce Disney publications.

From 1933 onwards Goofy — then still known as Dippy — appeared in many Mickey Mouse books as a member of the gang. An interesting curiosity is the 1938 publication, *Story of Dippy the Goof* (Whitman). This was the only book to feature Goofy in the intermediate stage of his Dippy Dawg — Dippy the Goof — Goofy sequence of identities.

In 1939, Goofy burst into print under his own name with *Goofy and Wilbur* (Whitman), the book of his first film as a solo star (see page 31 for the plot).

In England, Dean & Son of London produced *Mickey Mouse Annuals* from the early 1930s. In these, Goofy features as a major character in stories, jokes and poems. Because English artists were drawing the pictures, however, Goofy appeared as Dippy Dawg long after Art Babbitt and Floyd Gottfredson had established the classic Goofy on screen and in comic strips in the 1930s.

Today, Goofy is still going strong in hardcover books. *Goofy Annuals* are published in England by London Editions Ltd. and in France by Whitman-France. In Italy, Mondadori publishes Goofy adventures.

Goofy's popularity as a storybook character was matched by his success in the realms of the comic strip and comic book. It was here that his real development in print took place. January 1933 marked his first appearance in a syndicated Disney newspaper strip. Over 50 years later, he still appears in comic books and comic strips published in 14 languages and 15 countries.

A Christmas party at Mickey's house
Was a signal for oodles of fun,
And all of the gang arrived with gifts,
Which were opened one by one.

Copyright WALT DISNEY PRODUCTIONS, LTD., 1935

The cuckoo clock that Goofy got
Popped out, and laid him flat!
It would have knocked him silly,
But he was already that.

Horace is so swelled with pride
That he will squander his last dollar
For a picture, which would be
A handsome group: Himself and collar.

Goofy was given his own series of one-shot comic-book adventures in 1953. Many of these featured his fearsomely intelligent nephew, Gilbert. By 1965, Goofy was going from strength to strength. That year, he donned the cape and red flannel combinations of "Super Goof," a crime-fighting superhero powered by a mutant strain of goober nuts discovered growing on his own homestead.

Since then, he has also starred in comic-book spoofs of historical characters, literary and actual, including Rip van Winkle, Baron Frankenstein, Galileo and Leonardo da Vinci.

Goofy's career in comic strips and comic books helped further promote an already consistently rich and surprising comic persona. Both graphically and as a character, Goofy presents a wider range of possibilities to the comic-strip artist than either Mickey or Donald. His chaotic anatomy, which usually proceeds in several directions at once, brings an extra liveliness to the comic-book frame. He is always good for a pratfall or banana-skin gag and pantomime comedy in general.

As a comic-strip character, Goofy may miss the point entirely, creating funny situations. Or in his hit-or-miss fashion, he may go straight to the heart of things by means of an unexpected reaction. Either way, his screwball logic and personality enables crazy, hilarious things to happen all around him.

When paired with Goofy, Mickey tends to function as a straight man, a role very much in keeping with his popular image as an upright citizen. Donald Duck's short-fuse temperament is best displayed in brief, explosive slapstick. By comparison, Goofy's spiraling, slow-burn antics allow for a more extended storyline. All in all, it is fair to predict that Goofy will continue to enjoy a career as perhaps the most contemporary of the Disney comic-strip characters.

During the 1930s, Goofy was still developing as a personality. This book, issued by Whitman in 1938, was the first publication devoted exclusively to Goofy. However, its title suggests there was still some confusion in people's minds between the old Dippy Dawg and the contemporary Goofy.

As mentioned on page 13, Floyd Gottfredson, widely acknowledged as the dean of the Disney comic-strip artists, was largely responsible for the first comic-strip appearances of Goofy (or Dippy as he was then known).

Gottfredson took over the King Features syndicated black-and-white daily newspaper Mickey Mouse strips on May 5, 1930. This was just 5 months after they had been started by Ub Iwerks and Walt Disney. For the first 2 years he worked on the strips, Gottfredson both wrote and illustrated the stories.

From 1932 onward, Gottfredson was joined by a team of staff writers and artists. From then Gottfredson only provided the rough outline manuscript of each daily strip, which was polished and drawn up by other members of the team. Even so, his influence on both story and dialogue can be clearly seen. For several years Gottfredson also worked on the Mickey Mouse Sunday color strip, which began to appear in 1932.

He continued to be closely involved in the Mickey Mouse comic strips until his retirement in 1975.

Both Sunday and daily strips provided a series of extended Mickey Mouse adventures, each lasting about 3 months. After 1945, each strip — both daily and Sunday — became a self-contained episode. Gottfredson's prewar Mickey stories are now highly valued as classics of their kind. They are fast-paced, spiked with many twists and turns of plot and furnished with the hard-boiled, pithy dialogue of the Hollywood B-movies of the 1930s — police thrillers, gangster stories and tales of high adventure.

Goofy, still known as Dippy Dawg, was introduced in the newspaper strip at Walt Disney's suggestion. The first story in which he appeared was *Mickey Mouse and the Terrible Bandit Wolf Barker*, published in January 1933. This was also the first Sunday-comics story written entirely by Gottfredson.

Visually, Dippy was shown as a young dog, complete with tail and wearing a partial outfit consisting of waistcoat, hat, gloves and shoes. This characterization lasted until 1936, when Gottfredson added the familiar sweater and patched, long trousers to Dippy's wardrobe and gave him a different, but still old, pair of shoes. The new Dippy — now rechristened Goofy — was also a discernible step closer to the human species. Dippy had acquired elbows and knee joints, and his tail had disappeared.

The all-new Goofy was first seen, briefly, in the comic-strip story *Mickey Mouse and the Great Ostrich Race* (1936), and soon after in *Mickey Mouse and the Seven Ghosts*, also published in 1936. He made guest appearances in other Disney comic strips too, notably Al Taliaferro's Donald Duck Sunday comic strip.

Originally, Dippy's barnyard appearance in the comic strips was matched by his personality — that of an

Left: More Goofy comic capers, featuring the maestro's own brand of screwball logic. These self-contained Mickey Mouse Sunday comic strips from the late 1930s and early 1940s vividly illustrate another important aspect of Goofy's personality — his physical energy. He may go about it all wrong, but it's usually too late to stop him, which may account for the dazed expressions on the faces of his friends and neighbors! Top left: December 12, 1937. Bottom left: August 7, 1938. Center: February 15, 1942.

Above and bottom right: Goofy scenes from the comic-strip adventure, *Mickey Mouse and the Great Ostrich Race* (1936).

exuberant yokel, with a pretty basic sense of humor and an aversion to hard work.

Clarabelle Cow, in particular, clearly regards him as an unwelcome reminder of her own barnyard origins. And when we discover that Dippy's idea of a joke is to feed an elephant candy spiked with red pepper, we can of course see her point of view.

But, as we have seen, in the story *Mickey Mouse and the Terrible Bandit Wolf Barker*, published in 1933, Dippy saves Clarabelle, among others, from a stagecoach hold-up and, at the end of the story, defuses a potential quarrel between Clarabelle and Horace Horsecollar. While both episodes are due more to luck than judgment, they point to the existence of Goofy's good nature under the hayseed.

In *Mickey Mouse the Detective*, published in 1933-34, we discover to our astonishment that Dippy is a man of property with wealthy connections. When his rich detective uncle dies in the course of professional duties, he leaves the business to Dippy. That's the good news. The bad news is that he leaves his money to charity! At Mickey's suggestion, he and Dippy go into partnership, their slogan being "Sleuthing done dirt cheap." But Dippy is an unreliable business partner. Their first case is to find some stolen furniture, and Dippy proves to be the culprit!

In *Mickey Mouse and the Seven Ghosts* (1936), Goofy seems to have outgrown the delinquent, Dippy side of his personality. Mickey has returned from an adventure to discover the entire town — including Police Chief O'Hara — terrorized by a multiple haunting. Only Goofy is unperturbed, having had a number of interesting conversations with one of the ghosts. "A

swell guy, even if he has been dead for 400 years," in the estimation of Goofy, who is all for a live-and-let-haunt approach.

Mickey thinks otherwise and sets up a detective ghost-hunting agency to rid the town of the shadow of fear. His partners are Goofy and Donald, and their first client is none other than Colonel Bassett, owner of the haunted mansion. A patrician Southerner of the old school, Colonel Bassett has come to a horrible conclusion: "I realized, suh, that I have been entertaining ghosts that are not those of gentlemen!"

In this story, Goofy — complete with deerstalker hat and meerschaum pipe — is fully established in his new character as Mickey's slow-witted but eternally amiable sidekick. He plays a vital role in keeping the ghosts talking while Mickey is off investigating their real identity.

Goofy also shares in the reward when the "ghosts" are finally unmasked as smugglers and marched off to jail. Mickey, who was not above tossing Dippy Dawg out onto the street for irritating behavior, is now more protective toward Goofy, offering to look after his reward money.

At the end of the story, we see yet another side to Goofy's character — the romantic. With part of his money Goofy buys a new suit and is overwhelmed by the difference it makes. "When I look at myself in the mirror in my new suit an' I see how purty I look, it jest makes me feel like cryin'," he confides. But he only wears it for a day. When Minnie asks to see the new outfit, Goofy is bashful. For a long time, it seems, he's been hoping that one day the right girl would come along "an' if she did, I-huh-I-I wanted tuh save it for mah weddin'!"

Between 1938 and 1942, Goofy participated in seven major Mickey comic-strip adventures. He was Mickey's loyal shipmate aboard a whaler in *Mickey Mouse, Mighty Whalehunter,* published in 1938. Then he had a walk-on part in Mickey's first encounter with the menacing *Phantom Blot,* published in 1939. He dressed up as a gun-toting, singing cowboy in *Mickey and the Dude Ranch Bandit,* published in 1940, and was beaned by a prehistoric man in *Mickey Mouse on Cave Man Island,* published in 1940-41.

In 1942, in *Mickey Mouse in the Jewel Robbery,* Goofy was instrumental in capturing the notorious high-society jewel thief known as The Gleam, whose practice it was to hypnotize witnesses into forgetting what they had seen. Fortunately, the very special quality of Goofy's mind rendered him impervious to the hypnotic powers of the criminal. In the same year, Goofy took a break from adventure, to be Mickey's aide again, in an affair of the heart, entitled *Mickey Mouse in Love Trouble.*

With America drawn into World War II, Goofy volunteered for the Army but failed

Left: Mickey Mouse led the way for worldwide Disney character merchandising publications. Goofy appears on this 1936 cover of the British *Mickey Mouse Weekly* (left), which shows Mickey in a familiar role as a band leader. This British children's Disney newspaper from the early 1930s (center) was sponsored by a breakfast-cereal manufacturer.

Goofy finally appeared in his own comic book in 1953 — the last of the gang of three to establish his own one-shot series. Right and below right: Two examples published under Dell Four-Color Comics imprint.

the physical on three counts (reversed arches, concave chest and prolapsed abdomen). He was also rejected for defense work (low IQ). Undaunted, he managed to get a job with Mickey, who was too young and too short to serve, on a farm to help the war effort. Here again, the friends were soon back on the adventure trail, tracking down a bizarre saboteur — the episode is recounted in the story of *Mickey Mouse and the Black Crow Mystery*, published in 1942.

The saboteur, disguised as a huge black crow, proves not to be an enemy agent but an embittered former vegetable farmer out to avenge a humiliating defeat in the prize vegetable section of the local county fair. Clearly a poor loser, he had assaulted the winner with a butcher's knife and been sent to prison. There he'd hatched his evil plan to ruin all the farmers in the neighborhood. When released, he begins a campaign of arson and machinery-wrecking, culminating in an attempt to blow up the local dam. The scheme is foiled in the nick of time by Mickey.

This story is interesting for its blend of wartime atmosphere and rural nostalgia. It serves to illustrate that the farmers, greatest victims of the Depression years, were not seen by many as vital to the war effort. The Army guards the dam, but rural America is still a place where friendliness and neighborliness are the rule — a symbol of what Americans are fighting for.

In one sense, Goofy and Mickey have returned to their roots in the story, but they realize the country is no longer home. So they return to city life when, with the harvest in and the villain behind bars, their war work is over for the time being.

After the war, the daily and Sunday comic strips no longer featured long, serialized adventures. These were discontinued as a result of changes in the editorial policy of the newspapers which published them. However, many of the

Below: In 1955, this Dell comic-book, *Goofy Success Story*, chronicled the rise of Goofy, shy superstar.

Below right: In 1965 Super Goof — Goofy's crime-fighting alter ego — became a surprising extension of his personality. Even if Goofy's super mental powers leave him at the lower end of the superhero IQ range, people sleep more soundly knowing Super Goof is protecting them against criminals who threaten society.

prewar newspaper stories were redrawn and collected in the Disney comic books — strips and stories published in a magazine format.

Disney started producing comic books on a regular basis in 1940, following the enormous popularity of comic-book heroes, such as Superman, who first appeared in the late 1930s. The first comic-book publication, *Walt Disney's Comics and Stories*, grew swiftly. The initial issue in October 1940 had a print run of only 252,000 copies, but by August 1943 the print order was 1 million copies. In the peak year of 1952, the September issue reached 3.1 million copies. Beginning in 1948, this comic-book series was labeled as Dell Comics, and in 1962, continued as Gold Key Comics, and in 1980 as Whitman Comics.

From 1940 on another series of comic books published as Dell Four-Color Comics, featured Disney characters. Occasional issues were devoted to single Disney characters and later some of these "one-shots" developed into series of their own.

Goofy was a late recruit to the ranks of the one-shot comic-book heroes, although he was a regular and familiar guest in the 29

Mickey Mouse comic books published under the Dell Four-Color Comics imprint between 1941 and 1952.

Goofy's first one-shot comic book was Dell Four-Color Comic No. 468, published in 1953. Over the following 10 years, 15 more Goofy one-shots appeared. Then there was a 3-year absence before Goofy revealed himself as the amiable crimebuster "Super Goof" in 1965. To date, 74 Super Goof issues have been published.

For anyone interested in further research on Goofy, the following comic books are important. Dell Four-Color Comic No. 702, *Goofy Success Story*, recounts the full history of Goofy's rise from obscurity to stardom. Gold Key *Super Goof* No. 1 documents the first-ever transformation of Goofy into his crime-fighting secret identity.

Like Mickey and Donald, Goofy is also popular worldwide and goes by different names in the 14 languages in which his adventures appear. In Italy he is *Pippo*, in Norway *Langbein*, while Yugoslavia knows him as *Silja*. In France, he used to go by the name of *Dingo*, but today he is back to plain Goofy.

His appeal is as universal as Mickey's and Donald's but of a rather different kind. In the international Disney merchandising operation, Mickey and Donald have always been the torch-carriers, and symbols of the Disney enterprise. Goofy, though instantly recognizable, is less immediately definable than his cohorts.

At the same time, nearly all cultures have a rich store of folk tales and legends concerning amiable simpletons who make simple things complicated, and vice versa. In the words of Jack Kinney: "Goofy is Mr. Common Man. People can sympathize with him because that's not them, that's somebody else being crazy." Goofy as Everyman? That's as good a reason for Goofy's appeal as we're likely to get.

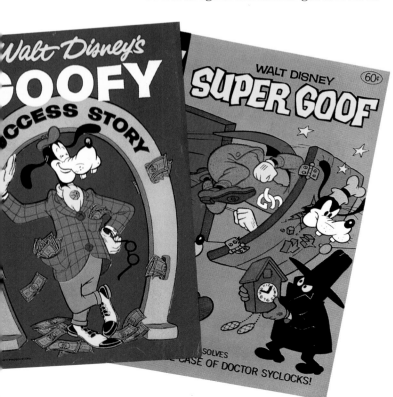

RETURN OF THE GOOF

GOOFY TODAY

Below and right: In 1983, Goofy came out of retirement to play the ghost of Jacob Marley in *Mickey's Christmas Carol*. In this Disney version of Dickens' immortal classic, Scrooge McDuck takes the part of Ebenezer Scrooge. Mickey plays Scrooge's impoverished clerk, Bob Cratchit.

Today, the Goof is once more firmly back in the public eye. Naturally, his absence from the screen in recent years had prompted rumors of a possible retirement. Perhaps Goofy the actor had decided it was time to concentrate on his public role as responsible elder statesman, greeting guests at Disneyland, Walt Disney World, and Tokyo Disneyland and helping out in educational projects. There has also been his deep involvement in the world of publishing — comics, books and newspaper strips — all of which must have kept him busy.

Fortunately, all the rumors and speculations were wrong. Today, Goofy's career is not merely ticking along, it's expanding again. The year 1984 saw Goofy make a comeback as an actor on the big screen, and he's recently become a sports superstar (as described overleaf).

Not surprising if you think about it.

With his old movies being regularly revived on the Disney TV Channel — introduced by literary sportsman George Plimpton — it was inevitable that he would be called back for further screen roles.

In the 1983 featurette *Mickey's Christmas Carol*, Goofy plays the ghost of Scrooge McDuck's dead partner Jacob Marley. Remembering Goofy's previous experience as a ghost *hunter* ("I ain't afraid of no ghosts") in *Lonesome Ghosts* (1937), this seems at first a strange reversal. And when, on a snowy Christmas Eve, Scrooge McDuck finds the ghostly head of Marley in place of his door-knocker, it's undoubtedly an extremely creepy moment. But the instant we recognize the noble features of a ghostly Goofy, we begin to suspect comedy.

As the miserly Scrooge mounts the stairs we see the shadow of Goofy, festooned with Marley's ghostly accouterments of chains, cashboxes and keys, creeping — rather awkwardly — after him. Then, with a crash, Goofy overbalances and falls downstairs.

Finally, he makes it to Scrooge's chamber to warn the wretch of the forthcoming visitations of the ghosts of Christmas Past, Christmas Present and Christmas Future. Even here he trips heavily over Scrooge's walking cane and takes another tumble. The blend of other-worldliness, humor and sympathy makes this cameo role a definitively Goofy performance. We can expect to see Goofy on the screen again soon — according to reliable sources.

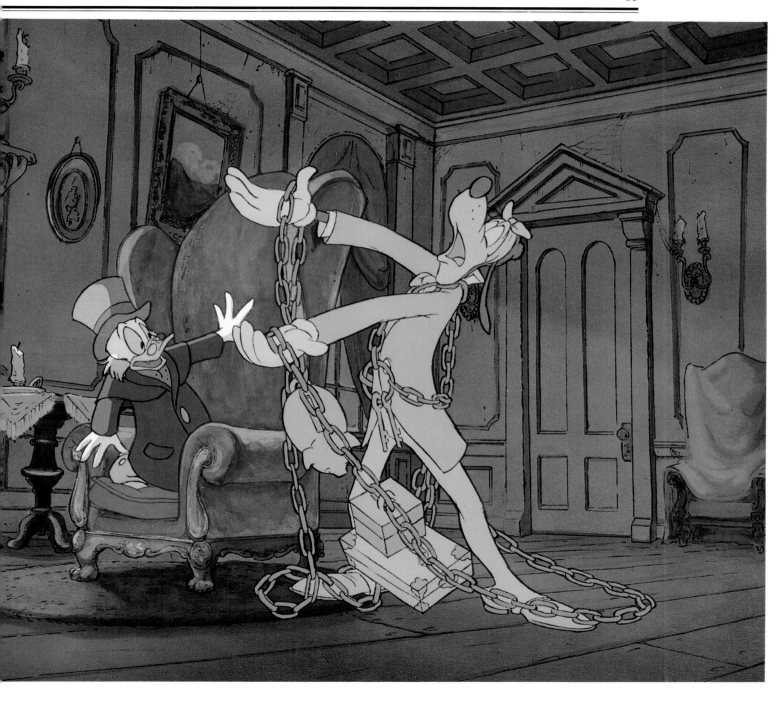

Studio model sheets plot the transformation of Goofy into Sport Goofy — dynamic 1980s star of the sporting world.

The year 1980 was a further milestone in Goofy's long and varied career. Within sight of his 50th birthday, this remarkable resilient character underwent another transformation. In the age of the physical fitness boom, this most unlikely of athletic superstars developed a new, muscular physique. With a firmer set of the jaw and a beadier eye, he burst upon the world as *Sport Goofy*.

Gone are the days when Goofy's hilarious attempts at all kinds of sports activities in the How-To films left him on the losing side. Now he's the much-respected official Walt Disney ambassador to the sporting world.

Sport Goofy grew out of the Disney organization's traditional commitment to youth. At the heart of everything Walt Disney stood for, was a profound belief in the imaginative, rich and fresh experience of childhood. The films and characters he created, his contributions to children's television entertainment and the famous theme parks at Disneyland, Walt Disney World, and Tokyo Disneyland are monuments to this belief.

In keeping with these values, the Disney organization has been sponsoring youth sports activities for many years, placing the emphasis on fun and enjoyment rather than competition.

Sport Goofy is the perfect symbol of this approach. He has a cheerful readiness to try anything once, and of course, some previous experience in a range of sports from his How-To films of the 1940s. He also seems to have retained his talent for althletic chaos.

In Sport Goofy's case, when his activities get a little off course, it has as much to do with overenthusiasm as with incompetence. His message to the world can be summed up as "Why worry if you're having fun?" And he does have fun. He unselfishly gives young people the confidence to try it anyway. They know

SPORT GOOFY GUIDELINES

DON'T OVERDO MUSCLES.

SPORT GOOFY NEVER WEARS A GOOFY HAT, VEST OR HARD SHOES.

SPORT GOOFY CAN BE A WINNER...

that however great their sporting goofs, Sport Goofy can goof one better.

In 1980, Sport Goofy made an international impact when the French Olympic team selected him as its mascot. He has also been officially endorsed by the German Sport Association. Now the Sport Goofy trophy attracts junior contestants, aged 14 and under, from more than 60

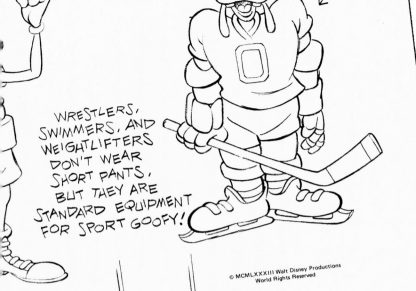

PADDING IS OKAY.

WRESTLERS, SWIMMERS, AND WEIGHTLIFTERS DON'T WEAR SHORT PANTS, BUT THEY ARE STANDARD EQUIPMENT FOR SPORT GOOFY!

[B]UT HE SHOULD [N]OT BE TAKEN [T]O SERIOUSLY!

[BOD]Y COMPARISON

SMALLER
[T]O COMPENSATE

[FE]ET AT A SLIGHTLY
[L]ESS ENERGY
[A]RE SMALLER,

[GR]OOMED.

HE HAS A SPORTIER "HAIRDO"

SMALLER LOWER CHIN

THE MOUTH IS NOT USUALLY DRAWN OFF TO THE SIDE IN A 3/4 VIEW.

SPORT GOOFY'S TEETH AREN'T TOO LONG.

Below and right: Sport Goofy is the perfect symbol of the Olympian ideal. This can be summarized as, "join in, have fun and aim to win a few." As the presiding spirit of an International Tennis Federation trophy competition for junior players Sport Goofy does his modest bit to inspire and encourage young sportsmen and sportswomen of all abilities.

countries in 20 tournaments around the world in the annual ITF (International Tennis Federation) Junior World Tennis Championships.

Tennis was chosen as the first major Sport Goofy promotion because it is so popular with both boys and girls — and because Disney Productions has a history of promoting the game. In Sweden during the 1960s, one contestant, Björn Borg, made quite an impression when he won what was then the "Kalle Anka" (Donald Duck) trophy.

More recently, the Disney people became concerned that junior tennis competitions might be getting a little too high-pressured. So in 1982 Disney, in association with the International Tennis Federation (the London-based parent organization of world tennis) sponsored a Sport Goofy invitation tournament for young players from the 14 and under, and 12 and under age-groups.

Both the standard of play and the relaxed sporting atmosphere made the event a resounding success. It seemed that Sport Goofy's message — take part, have fun, aim to win a few rather than winning

them all — could get through to today's young sports competitors.

In 1985, Sport Goofy, with his famous grin, will be presiding over a wide range of sports tournaments, competitions and events — local, regional and national — in the United States, Europe and elsewhere. Sports include tennis, soccer, golf, basketball, winter sports, ice hockey, cycling, hang gliding and swimming.

In the United States, Sport Goofy is closely involved with the National Federation of State High School Associations in a special program to promote high school track and field events.

With a full schedule of television specials, personal appearances, and an upcoming series of cartoon shorts, Sport Goofy promises to become the most widely known sporting character of the 1980s. His first film, presently titled *Soccer Mania*, will probably be released with a full-length animated feature in late 1985. Meanwhile, he is already on video in a "package" accompanying his 1981 song *You Can Always Be Number One,* the Sport Goofy anthem.

In this latest dynamic phase, Goofy is

adding further prestige to a career in which, at every stage, he has never ceased to surprise his audiences. Belying his early reputation as the lightweight background comic of the Disney characters, Goofy has shown astonishing powers of survival and renewal.

He's always been in the right place at the right time, whether it was the change from early puppetlike animation to the lifelike animation of the 1930s, the "new look" for 1940s-style cartoon capers or the charting of 1950s suburban consciousness.

In the course of his long career, Goofy has worked with some of the greatest names in animation — Walt Disney, Art Babbitt, Woolie Reitherman, Mickey Mouse and Donald Duck. All praise him. And, although he has made fewer film appearances than Mickey or Donald, Goofy's face is known throughout the world.

It's a remarkable story. But, in the end, the mystery at its heart is really no mystery at all. Through all his changes, Goofy has simply remained true to the rich personality that Art Babbitt first created for him in 1935. He is a character who finds life endlessly complicated, but never threatening, who thinks long and hard before doing the wrong thing. His catastrophes are comic but never fatal, and his good nature helps him rise above every obstacle. By doing things wrong, but not minding, Goofy lets us recognize every dumb thing we've ever done — but with laughter rather than irritation.

Goofy's most enduring message to all of us is that brains may be one thing, but the philosophical good-humor needed to handle the wild cards dealt by a mischievous Fate is just as important. His survival for more than 50 years is adequate proof that Goofy's approach, however crazy, may be right after all. Goofy, endearing and enduring star of the cartoon screen, we salute you!

FILMOGRAPHY

The following comprehensive filmography lists the shorts, features and commercial films in which Goofy has appeared. The names of the directors of these productions are given in brackets. Goofy has also appeared in a number of Disney television shows.

1932
Mickey's Revue (Mickey Mouse cartoon. Wilfred Jackson)
The Whoopee Party (Mickey Mouse cartoon. Wilfred Jackson)
Touchdown Mickey (Mickey Mouse cartoon. Wilfred Jackson)
The Klondike Kid (Mickey Mouse cartoon. Wilfred Jackson)

1933
Mickey's Mellerdrammer (Mickey Mouse cartoon. Wilfred Jackson)
Ye Olden Days (Mickey Mouse cartoon. Bert Gillett)

1934
Orphan's Benefit (Mickey Mouse cartoon. Bert Gillett)

1935
The Band Concert (Mickey Mouse cartoon. Wilfred Jackson)
Mickey's Service Station (Mickey Mouse cartoon. Ben Sharpsteen)
Mickey's Fire Brigade (Mickey Mouse cartoon. Ben Sharpsteen)
On Ice (Mickey Mouse cartoon. Ben Sharpsteen)

1936
Mickey's Polo Team (Mickey Mouse cartoon. Dave Hand)
Moving Day (Mickey Mouse cartoon. Ben Sharpsteen)

1937
Moose Hunters (Mickey Mouse cartoon. Ben Sharpsteen)
Hawaiian Holiday (Mickey Mouse cartoon. Ben Sharpsteen)
Clock Cleaners (Mickey Mouse cartoon. Ben Sharpsteen)
Lonesome Ghosts (Mickey Mouse cartoon. Bert Gillett)
Magician Mickey (Mickey Mouse cartoon. Dave Hand)
Mickey's Amateurs (Mickey Mouse cartoon. Pinto Colvig, Walt Pfeiffer, Ed Penner)

1938
Boat Builders (Mickey Mouse cartoon. Ben Sharpsteen)
Mickey's Trailer (Mickey Mouse cartoon. Ben Sharpsteen)
The Whalers (Mickey Mouse cartoon. Dick Huemer)
Polar Trappers (Donald Duck and Goofy cartoon. Ben Sharpsteen)
The Fox Hunt (Donald Duck and Goofy cartoon. Ben Sharpsteen)

1939
Goofy and Wilbur (Dick Huemer. First cartoon to star Goofy)

1940
Billposters (Donald Duck cartoon. Clyde Geronimi)
Tugboat Mickey (Mickey Mouse cartoon. Clyde Geronimi)
Goofy's Glider (Jack Kinney)

1941
Baggage Buster (Jack Kinney)
The Art of Skiing (Jack Kinney)
The Art of Self Defense (Jack Kinney)
The Nifty Nineties (Mickey Mouse cartoon. Riley Thomson)
How to Ride a Horse (Sequence from *The Reluctant Dragon*, released theatrically as a cartoon short in 1950. Jack Kinney)
Orphan's Benefit (Mickey Mouse cartoon, color remake. Riley Thomson)

1942
Mickey's Birthday Party (Mickey Mouse cartoon. Riley Thomson)
Symphony Hour (Mickey Mouse cartoon. Riley Thomson)
How to Play Baseball (Jack Kinney)
The Olympic Champ (Jack Kinney)
How to Swim (Jack Kinney)
How to Fish (Jack Kinney)

1943
Victory Vehicles (Jack Kinney)
El Gaucho Goofy (sequence of *Saludos Amigos*, released theatrically as a cartoon short in 1955. Jack Kinney)

1944
How to Be a Sailor (Jack Kinney)
How to Play Golf (Jack Kinney)
How to Play Football (Academy Award nomination. Jack Kinney)

1945
Tiger Trouble (Jack Kinney)
African Diary (Jack Kinney)
Californy 'er Bust (Jack Kinney)
Hockey Homicide (Jack Kinney)
No Sail (Donald Duck and Goofy cartoon. Jack Hannah)

1946
A Knight for a Day (Jack Hannah)
Double Dribble (Jack Hannah)
Frank Duck Brings 'em Back Alive (Donald Duck and Goofy cartoon. Jack Hannah)

1947
Crazy with the Heat (Donald Duck and Goofy cartoon. Charles Nichols)
Foul Hunting (Jack Hannah)
Mickey and the Beanstalk (sequence of *Fun and Fancy Free*. Bill Roberts)

1948
They're Off (Jack Hannah)
The Big Wash (Clyde Geronimi)

1949
Tennis Racquet (Jack Kinney)
Goofy Gymnastics (Jack Kinney)

1950
Motor Mania (Jack Kinney)
Crazy Over Daisy (Donald Duck cartoon. Jack Hannah)
Hold That Pose (Jack Kinney)

1951
Lion Down (Jack Kinney)
Home Made Home (Jack Kinney)
Cold War (Jack Kinney)
Tomorrow We Diet (Jack Kinney)
Get Rich Quick (Jack Kinney)
Fathers Are People (Jack Kinney)
No Smoking (Jack Kinney)

1952
Father's Lion (Jack Kinney)
Hello Aloha (Jack Kinney)
Man's Best Friend (Jack Kinney)
Two Gun Goofy (Jack Kinney)
Teachers Are People (Jack Kinney)
Two Weeks Vacation (Jack Kinney)
How to Be a Detective (Jack Kinney)

1953
Father's Day Off (Jack Kinney)
Father's Week End (Jack Kinney)
For Whom the Bulls Toil (Jack Kinney)
How to Dance (Jack Kinney)
How to Sleep (Jack Kinney)

1961
Aquamania (Woolie Reitherman)

1965
Freewayphobia No. 1 (Les Clark)
Goofy's Freeway Trouble (Les Clark)

1983
Mickey's Christmas Carol (Mickey Mouse featurette. Academy Award nomination. Burny Mattinson)

BIBLIOGRAPHY

The following bibliography represents a small but classic selection of other publications on Goofy and the world of Disney.

Bailey, Adrian, *Walt Disney's World of Fantasy* (1982, Everest House, New York/ Paper Tiger, London)

Canemaker, John, "Art Babbitt, the Animator as Firebrand" (September, 1975, *Millimeter, III*)

Canemaker, John, "Art Babbitt" (December, 1979, *Cartoonist Profiles*, No 44)

Canemaker, John, (Introduction), *Treasures of Disney Animation Art* (1982, Abbeville Press, New York)

Feild, Robert D, *The Art of Walt Disney* (1942/4, Macmillan, New York/ Collins, London and Glasgow)

Finch, Christopher, *The Art of Walt Disney — From Mickey Mouse to the Magic Kingdoms* (1973, Harry N. Abrams, New York)

Gottfredson, Floyd, (Introduction), *Walt Disney's Mickey Mouse — Best Comics* (1978, Abbeville Press, New York)

Kinney, Jack, "Bambi and the Goof" (Fall, 1979, *Funnyworld* No 21)

Maltin, Leonard, *Of Mice and Magic: A History of American Animated Cartoons* (1980, McGraw Hill, New York)

Munsey, Cecil, *Disneyana: Walt Disney Collectibles* (1974, Hawthorn, New York)

Schroeder, Horst, (Introduction), *Walt Disney's Goofy — Best Comics* (1979 Abbeville Press, New York)

Shale, Richard, "Donald Duck Joins Up — The Walt Disney Studio during World War II" (Fall 1977, *Funnyworld* No 17 and 1982, UMI Research Press, Ann Arbor, Michigan)

Thomas, Frank and Johnston, Ollie, *Disney Animation — The Illusion of Life* (1981, Abbeville Press, New York)

SPORT GOOFY DIARY

In 1980, Goofy underwent an amazing transformation to become Sport Goofy, the official Walt Disney ambassador to the sporting world.

The following chronology lists the major events in Sport Goofy's diary of the last few years.

1932
Goofy's film debut in *Mickey's Revue*.

1940
Goofy begins his classic "How-To" film series featuring skiing, glider flying, basketball, baseball, football and other sports.

1968
Sweden inaugurates its national junior tennis program. The winner is 13-year-old Björn Borg.

1980
Goofy is named official mascot of the French Olympic Team, with the title "Sport Goofy."

1980
Brazil stages a Sport Goofy mini-Olympiad in Rio de Janeiro. The competition is watched by 60,000 spectators.

1981
Germany names Sport Goofy the spokesman for the German Sportlife Fund.

1981
Sport Goofy tours major football events in Germany, France and England with his Adidas professional football player friends.

1981
Sport Goofy appears in Disney magazines throughout Europe as "Disney's Ambassador" to the world of sports.

1983
Sport Goofy rides in the Pace Car at the Indianapolis 500 motor race. The Goodyear Blimp circles above, featuring his image.

1983
Wimbledon International Tennis Federation announces the first ITF Junior World Tennis Championship, "The Sport Goofy Trophy," to be held at Walt Disney World.

1983
Sport Goofy runs in the New York Marathon.

1983
10,000 fans greet Sport Goofy in Peru, where he hosts a major national sports festival.

1983
National Sport Goofy youth programs begin in United Kingdom, France, Japan, Argentina, Brazil, Canada, Spain, Denmark, Hong Kong and Peru.

1983
39 nations participate in the ITF Junior World Tennis Championships, "The Sport Goofy Trophy," at Walt Disney World. Stan Smith awards sportsmanship trophy.

1983
Sport Goofy is named the "Official National Mascot of High School Sports" in North America.

1983
Sport Goofy is featured at Bath, in England, during the national British Tennis Championship and Disney Sports Celebration.

1983
Sport Goofy launches his own TV show, *Mickey and Donald present Sport Goofy*, in 36 countries.

1984
Sport Goofy stars in the halftime extravaganza at the United States Professional Football Championships, "The Superbowl." This is seen by 100 million TV viewers.

1984
Scotland inaugurates the 12-nation "Sport Goofy Trophy" competition in Dundee.

1984
Brazil begins a national Sport Goofy football program. Sport Goofy is seen nationwide with the national team on a "fair play" national TV campaign.

1984
Portugal names Sport Goofy its Olympic mascot.

1984
Sport Goofy entertains all the Olympic Teams at Disneyland during the Los Angeles Olympic Games.

1984
Sport Goofy appears at French Open Tennis Championship.

1984
Sport Goofy leads the pack in Britain's world-famous cycle marathon, the "Milk Race."

1984
Sport Goofy Tennis Program expands to 70 nations, with 300,000 participants.

1984
The ITF Junior World Tennis Championship, "The Sport Goofy Trophy," hosts 49 nations at Walt Disney World.

1985
Second annual Sport Goofy International Hockey Trophy is shown on national TV in the United Kingdom. Participants come from 12 nations.

1985
Walt Disney Productions is planning new youth world sports championships in football, golf, sailboarding, bowling and basketball. Sport Goofy is to participate.

1985
Sport Goofy in *Soccer Mania*, a new cartoon to be premiered at the World Cup in Mexico.

1985
Goofy joins Linda Fratianne, Olympic Silver Medalist Ladies Figure Skating, 1980, and the all-star cast of *Disney on Ice* for a nationwide tour of 35 cities.

1985
Sport Goofy is a guest of honor at the U.S. Ski Team's Celebrity Classic. He is seen on ESPN, a major American sports TV network.

1985
Sport Goofy teams up with Adidas in San Diego, New York and Tampa at NASL playoff soccer matches. Special coaching sessions for youth soccer players are held at the stadiums before the matches.